FROM TIMOR-LESTE TO AUSTRALIA

SEVEN FAMILIES, THREE GENERATIONS TELL THEIR STORIES

EDITED BY

JAN TREZISE

Published by Wild Dingo Press
Melbourne, Australia
books@wilddingopress.com.au
www.wilddingopress.com.au

First published by Wild Dingo Press 2018

Designer: Michael Mysik
Editor: Catherine Lewis
Print in Australia by Griffin Press

Trezise, Jan, 1941 - editor.
From Timor-Leste to Australia / Jan Trezise.

A catalogue record for this book is available from the National Library of Australia

ISBN: 9780987381101 (paperback)
ISBN: 9780648215981 (ebook: pdf)
ISBN: 9780987381132 (ebook)

Jan Trezise grew up in Springvale South where successive groups of refugees and migrants settled in the surrounding areas. This early experience informed a lifelong activism in support of refugees.

Jan taught in both primary and secondary schools, and was the inaugural Principal of Gleneagles Secondary College in Endeavour Hills, Melbourne where many East Timorese families had settled. She has always been actively involved in her local community, welcoming and supporting refugees and migrants when the Enterprise Migrant Hostel was established in Springvale in 1970, setting up a program which linked local families to migrant families living in the hostel, later becoming a local councillor then the first female mayor of the City of Springvale.

Jan was president for 15 years of Friends of Ermera, founded in 2002 to provide educational training and mentorship in the District of Ermera. She has visited Timor-Leste many times, consulting with national and municipal education authorities, mentoring groups and individuals and assisting in the training of teachers.

This book is dedicated to the brave men, women, and children of Timor-Leste who lost their lives in the fight for the independence of their nation.

ACKNOWLEDGEMENTS

The inspiration for publishing this book came from the members of the seven families who have shared their personal journeys with us and particularly their long struggle for their nation's independence. We thank them for their time, honesty and openness. By allowing us to document their inspirational stories and providing us with copies of their unique family photos, they have made an important contribution to the recording of Timor-Leste and Australian history.

The initial interviews of the family members were conducted over several months by students from Gleneagles Secondary College, Endeavour Hills, Victoria. The students documented the stories and provided us with the raw manuscript for the book. Without the support of the school and the teachers involved, led by teacher Lynne Moller, the stories might never have been documented. The students involved in the project were: Humna Aamir; Tome Correia; Jess Fitzgerald; Charlie Holmes; Nick Ilic; Joshua Kumar; Nehareeka Kaur; Andrew Lakshamalia; Kimberley Lofthouse; Lily Lunder; Kaelen McKinnon; Keisha Nathan; Vishal Panditharatne; Erin Porteous; Krish Rajavel; Nikitha Ramkumar; Zacki Rizwan; Chelsea Roy; Viranya Samarasinghe; Gita (Tirtani) Santosa; Khushi Sharma; Sean Silva; Emily Song; Nick Stamatopolous; Naomi Yong.

More extensive interviews to further explore the stories were conducted by Jan Trezise who went on to develop the manuscript. We want to thank Merle Mitchell and Geoff Trezise who provided the first edits of the stories.

The excellent curriculum kit which accompanies this book and ensures that it becomes a valuable teaching resource in our secondary schools has been prepared by Lynne Moller and Marilyn Davidson.

Catherine Lewis from Wild Dingo Press recognised the potential of the book and it has been a pleasure to work with her as she guided us through the publishing process.

The City of Casey has an active friendship link with the municipality of Ermera in Timor-Leste and has provided the funds to publish this book along with the venues and their staff assistance to enable us to appropriately celebrate each milestone in the interviewing, documenting, sharing, and launching of the book.

Jan Trezise, Melbourne, 2018

Table of Contents

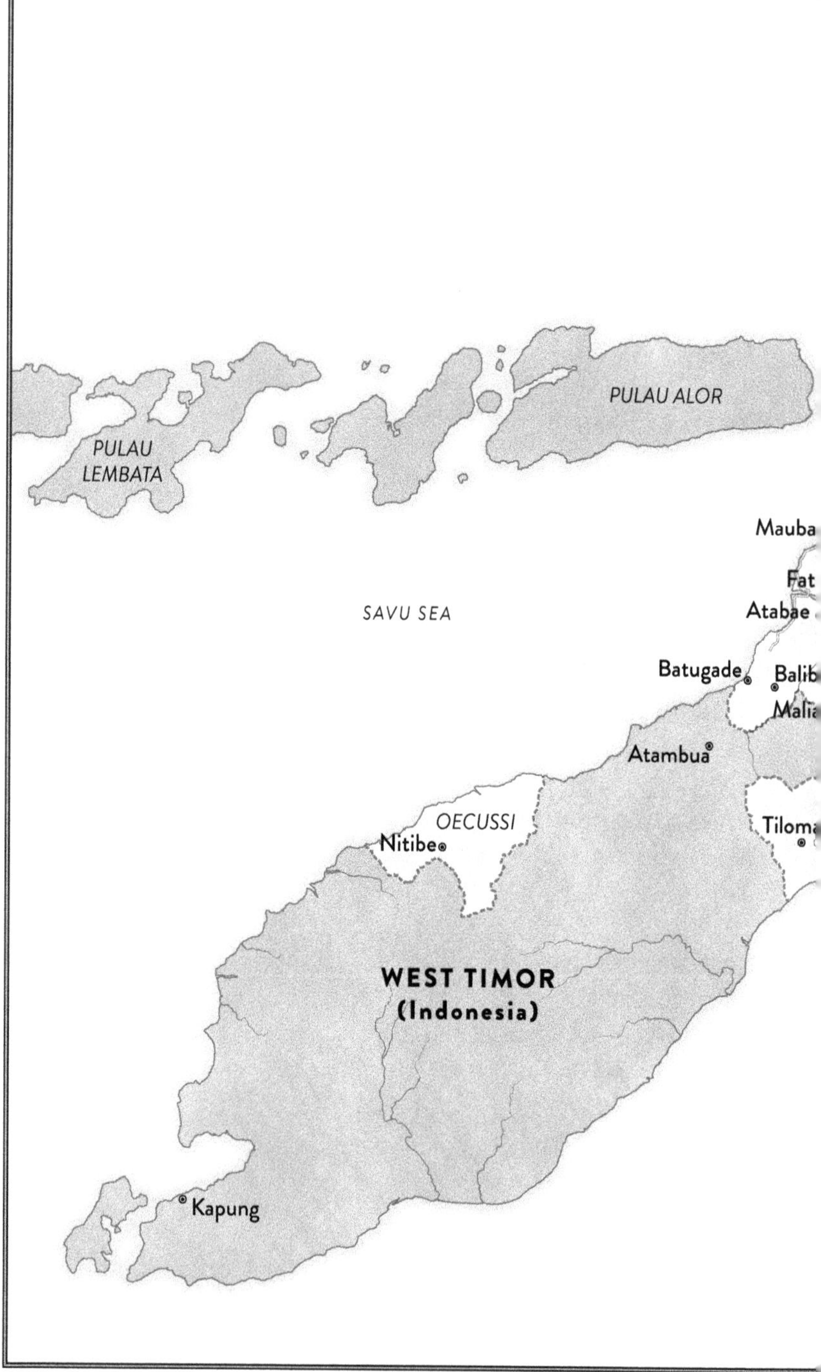
PULAU ALOR
PULAU
LEMBATA
SAVU SEA
Atabae
Batugade
Atambua
OECUSSI
Nitibe
WEST TIMOR
(Indonesia)
Kapung

BANDA SEA
PULAU WETAR
ATAURA ISLAND
Dili
Hera
Manatutu
Baucau
Dare
Rexexio
Aileu
Vila
TIMOR-LESTE
Ossu
Soibada
TIMOR SEA

N
0 20 40 km

Manila
PHILIPPINES
SOUTH
CHINA
SEA
MALYASIA
SINGAPORE
Jakarta
INDONESIA
Dili
TIMOR
LESTE
Da
INDIAN OCEAN
AU
Perth
N
0 200 400 600 800 1000 km

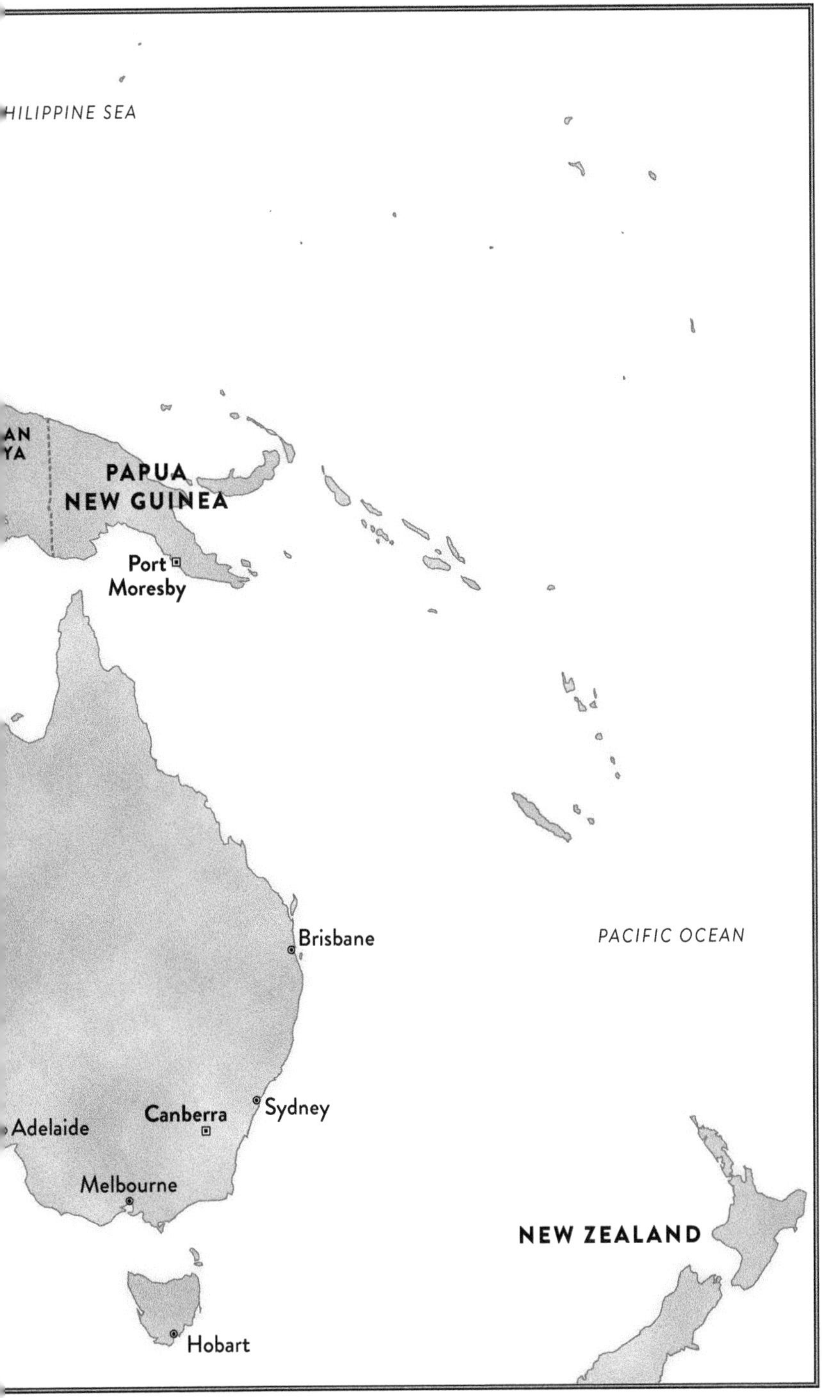

HILIPPINE SEA

AN
YA

PAPUA
NEW GUINEA

Port
Moresby

Brisbane

PACIFIC OCEAN

Sydney

Adelaide

Canberra

Melbourne

NEW ZEALAND

Hobart

Gomes Family

Amandio Gomes

When my father died and the war with Japan broke out in East Timor in 1942, I was very young and we were very poor. But my beliefs, along with the help of other people, allowed me to get through the tough times. It also helped that in East Timor everyone was friends.

I remember that at my school you had to cross a river to get to the college. Some people who were very clever called other people stupid, but they did not know how to cross the river. The people who were called stupid knew how to cross the river, and they would teach others; they were respected for this. So you see, you have to respect each other to have a good life because in one way or another, everyone has different kinds of knowledge.

I would like to ask you young people who are interviewing me today and will write my family story, that when you grow up, please love each other. Listen to each other and understand each other, have sympathy. If you don't, you will have an enemy everywhere you go and you will not be helped.

I am not wise—I just have experiences in life. So thank you for listening to me.

It is important to appreciate the history of East Timor and the fact that for centuries my country had been occupied by one foreign power or another. East Timor had been a Portuguese colony since the 16th century. Japan occupied Timor in 1942 and remained there until the end of World War 2 in 1945 when we returned to Portuguese rule once again. We were a Portuguese colony until 1975 when FRETLIN (Revolutionary Front for an independent East Timor) declared independence on 28 November 1975. Nine days later, Indonesia invaded.

In 1999 after 24 years of Indonesian occupation, the East Timorese were given the opportunity to vote for independence. They voted overwhelmingly in favour. In 2002 East Timor officially became an independent nation.

I was born in 1939 in Behau, Hatolia, a sub-district of Ermera in the south-western part of East Timor. My family was very poor, and my father passed away when I was about five years old, so my childhood was not easy. My family was poor because my parents were raising and supporting friends and relatives and other people who were having it tougher than us.

I went to primary school in Baucau but when the Japanese invaded Timor, my schooling was interrupted because we were forced to move from place to place around the island. My family finally settled in the capital Dili, and I continued my studies at Soibada College and then Dari Seminary. But at the age of 16 I had to stop as my family was struggling financially, so I found a job working as an interpreter with the Chinese-Timorese merchants.

During my time at school I had many great teachers but there was one Salesian priest, Father Abinal, who saw something in my curious mind that lead me to become a mechanic at first, then an electrician. It was Father Abinal who encouraged me to pull apart engines and motors to determine the fault, then to fix it, and re-assemble them again. It was also Father Abinal who guided me in the right direction.

My first real job was working for *Camara Municipal de Dili* (Municipal Offices) learning to work as a government official for local council. It was there that I came to realise that the Timorese were not given an equal opportunity, and that there was a huge disparity in salaries and responsibilities between Portuguese and Timorese workers. So I decided to quit my job and started working with another government agency dealing with imports and exports, but realised that here, too, the Timorese were not recognised as equals. I complained and became quite vocal in my workplace, which is how I started forming my political views towards Portuguese rule.

I worked with a few different companies in different roles but kept being drawn to electrical and mechanical work, where I developed a good reputation. As electricity was always intermittent in Dili, the government put out a tender to overseas companies to deliver power to Dili efficiently and reliably. An English company won the contract but there was no one in Timor who understood how to manage and maintain these particular generators. So Manuel Carrascalão, a man of influence in Dili, recommended me to the government and I ended up going to England for over a year to further my studies in electrical and mechanical repairs. I remember the meeting with him quite well. I was still quite young and was sitting quietly among Portuguese and Timorese workers. I am very thankful to Senhor Carrascalão who believed in me and trusted that I was capable of taking this huge opportunity.

Manuel Carrascalão had been a close friend of my father's and I am grateful that my father had such good friends who kept looking after me even though he had passed away so long ago. My father worked as a government official, and in that role helped many families so was well respected in the community. That's the thing about being Timorese: we look after each other. We understand the value and importance of community.

As for my competence in the English language, I had learnt that from an Australian couple who had retired to Dili after having lived there for many years during their working lives. At that time there were some Australians working out of Dili on the oil rigs as well as businesses that traded between Dili and Darwin. They were lovely people, and in exchange, I taught them Portuguese and Tetum.

Much later, I was approached by another friend of my father's, an Australian engineer who offered me work in an oil drilling company. Initially, I was in charge of maintenance of refrigerators and water pipes for oil drilling. But then I was given many roles and responsibilities in this company and was lucky to have good bosses who allowed me to use their machinery outside work hours. On my days off I would often take the tractors and tools and help the families in the community to build their houses and do general repairs.

This diary that follows, keeps track of what happened in my adult life as I remember the hardships, the laughter, the fear and the sadness of my life and the events that were happening in my homeland, my Timor-Leste.

September 1971

I sometimes despair for our future. My country should be our country, not someone else's! We must stick together, and we should be our *own* country! If Portugal recognised the Timorese as equals and we were given equal opportunities at work and study, then I think the Timorese would not be rebelling so much against the colonial power.

This was the year my youngest daughter, Carmelita, was born; so now we have another member of our family. My wife, Fatima, has had such difficulties with her pregnancy that I think it was a miracle that she and our daughter both survived. Fatima had a dream during the pregnancy of the Virgin Mary at the foot of her bed who said, 'You shall name her, Carmelita'. And so it was that Carmelita was born, joining her sister, Elizabete, the oldest. She was later followed by two brothers, Amandio and Bernardo—completing the Gomes family.

December 1971

Every day is tiresome. I am now working as a mechanic and machine operator in charge of keeping creeks and the sea clean, and today was no different. But when I arrived home, the sight of my beautiful darling wife, Fatima, and the smiles of my four children, somehow made my worries all go away. Their existence makes my days better—they support me; I adore them. As I sit in the rugged landscape of Timor and behold the stars, I wonder and reflect: *I love my family.*

March 1972

Today I vowed to myself to make my children's home a better place for them and for everyone! I don't want my children to go through what I did. The memories of my father passing away too soon and the extreme poverty we all experienced as children still haunts me. I remember it all just as if it was yesterday—the piercing coldness whenever the sun went away, my only source of heat vanishing—the deep grumble in my stomach, the realisation that I had no father to learn from, no father to look up to. Then I remembered that even though times were tough in my childhood, we worked as a family and community; everyone knew one another, and most importantly, everyone united together. Despite the awfulness of those times, I consider myself to be fortunate to have lived through them.

April 1972

Today, I finally mustered up enough courage to share my thoughts and my beliefs; I decided to pass on my opinions to others. As I prepared to share with my people, my family and fellow workers, I had a quick moment of panic and apprehension. Looking around hesitantly, I realised I was very nervous; but when my eyes focused on our community, the sight of our unity, our culture and our country, I was inspired. When I spoke, I found that I was not alone, that others, too, loved our country deeply and wanted independence from Portugal.

My letters to the Portuguese government authorities have been answered by a very demoralising letter. It reads:

Dear Amandio,

I am sure you are not happy to read this, but we have no interest in making Timor-Leste independent at any time in the future. Your words and thoughts do concern us as this country is and always will be a colony under Portuguese rule. If you have any further comments or questions, please write or visit us in Dili, where we can talk in person.

On Behalf of the Government of Portugal

To the Government of Portugal,
If Portugal is not interested in allowing Timor to become independent, then the Timorese people need to be given equal opportunities and chances. We are not your criados (servants) and we demand equal respect and consideration. We are a proud people and deserve a better chance in life.

I have read your letter but still believe that my people and my country should have a chance to become independent. Some families have older members who were brought here from Portugal, but now they and their families see themselves as Timorese. I was born in Timor; my grandfather was also born in Timor. We are Timorese. Why are we still Portuguese if we live in and love Timor-Leste?

Amandio

Week 1, April 1972

By the time I have finished attending to my wife and children, it is usually too dark for me to write anything productive. This night, I have put my children to bed earlier so that I now have time before it gets pitch black. The electricity keeps failing in Dili; I don't know when the government is going to get this basic service fixed. I won't be giving away what I know is the solution to this problem unless I'm recognised and paid accordingly. They don't really seem interested anyway. Every day, anger starts to well up in me as I think back to the answers I have received from the Portuguese Government.

Week 3, April 1972

I mutter and vow that everyone in Timor-Leste will be free, independent and treated equally by everyone. It is always the sound of my children that keeps me sane and happy. I make a promise to myself then to make sure my children never have to go through the same pains as I did through the hardship and struggles to keep our family alive and healthy. I have since received another two letters back from the Government of Portugal. I am so torn up about the last letter that I do not know how to respond. The letters and my reply follow.

Dear Amandio,
Your letters concern us, and we believe that you are confused. As this colony was founded by Portugal and is still being managed by the Portuguese, we do not see why it should become independent from Portugal. It is still under the rule of Portugal. We urge you to stop this nonsense immediately or we will need to act accordingly.

On Behalf of the Government of Portugal

To the Government of Portugal
I do hope to meet you in person to explain to you the reasons why my family and our friends believe in Timor-Leste as an independent country of love and laughter. We believe that no one is insignificant. People that you may consider 'dumb' may one day teach you something valuable. We believe that our people should have a chance to be free, a chance to manage our own country.

Amandio

Dear Amandio
You need to understand what we have told you several times: Timor-Leste will remain a Portuguese colony.

We have no interest in hearing your opinions and do not want to receive any more letters from you. To continue on this path will be detrimental to you and your family. Your views are not welcome or tolerated.

On Behalf of the Government of Portugal

Week 4, April 1972

This cannot be good. The authorities are upset by my views. I understood that my views were not appreciated by them and was aware that some Timorese had been imprisoned recently for the same beliefs. Still, I thought it important to continue to fight the government.

But one day I was approached by a Portuguese engineer who had connections with the army. He sympathised with my views and advised me of the danger I was facing. He made me realise the impact my imprisonment would have on my family; and informed me that the PIDE (International and State Defence Police) was watching me closely which meant that I risked ending up in prison.

And so it happened. I am being 'encouraged' to leave my country or face imprisonment for my political views. The authorities have told me that I have a day to pack before I must board a plane bound for Mozambique, another Portuguese colony, where I am to be exiled but not imprisoned. In haste, I decide to leave my family behind because we have not had time to make plans before I am to be expelled from my own country! It is dusk, and I have stolen some time in which to write this journal. I leave at sunrise tomorrow.

A possible escape plan forms in my mind: my flight takes me via Darwin where I have been offered a job with an Australian company.

My plan failed. As I landed in Darwin, I met a fellow-Timorese with whom I shared my plan, only to find out later that he notified the Australian police. At the time I thought he had betrayed me, but then I realised many years later when I migrated to Australia and met him again, that his actions were with good intentions: to save me from committing a crime against the Portuguese regime which also had contacts in Australia. And so I was found in Darwin and taken back on board the plane bound for Mozambique.

I managed, however, to jot down a few words while on the plane, exiled from my own country by some foreign and corrupt government. Feeling distraught at the time of departure, I felt that it was the end of the world and I couldn't help but feel guilty at the situation I put my family in. I had become interested in political action as a way of seeking a better future for my country, but unfortunately, my political views were not acceptable to the Portuguese authorities and became the reason for my exile.

What future am I providing for my family now? I think of my children and am reminded of my promise to keep them safe and make sure they don't ever have to experience the hardships and the loss of their father as I did. It also reminds me to be a good father and to be the good role model that I had wished my father could have been alive to provide to me.

I believed that a door may have been shut in our faces, but other doors will open and give us a chance. Hopefully, a new pathway will lead to a new future. Unfortunately, this time I had waved goodbye to my beloved country.

Upon my arrival in Mozambique, I had a visit from PIDE officers to make sure I had actually arrived and to ensure that

I fully understood my obligations including the requirement to report to the police every month about my work and my whereabouts.

May 1972

Now I need to work really hard to make sure my family is allowed to join me in Mozambique because I do not want them to be left behind without my support.

1972-1975

Mozambique is better than I expected. Our family is reunited and the company I work for has provided us with a nice home. I have met some other Timorese people who have also been exiled and we have managed to make some new friends. There is a lot of work for me as an electrician, and I really enjoy helping others in our new community. The people in Mozambique are very friendly and respectful—both qualities I admire. As my kids are young, they are just happy to play around. Seeing them happy makes me happy, and that cycle lives on.

Upon reflection, I remember that my maternal grandfather had also been exiled to Mozambique for wanting independence from Portugal. My mother tells me that he spent a few years in prison before being released to live in Mozambique. My grandfather is a descendant of the great Don Boaventura the *Liurai* of Same who led the famous rebellion against Portuguese rule, known as the Manufahi War of 1911-1912. So, it's in my blood.

My grandfather married an Indian/Mozambiquan woman and their two children, my mother and my uncle, were both born in Mozambique. The family later migrated to Timor after the Portuguese political rule became less oppressive, and some Timorese exiles were allowed to return.

My life in Mozambique turned out to be a great success because I was finally being recognised both financially and personally for my skills and experience. I had an important job working as an electrician, collaborating in the great Cahora Bassa power transmission system (the largest hydro-electric system in southern Africa) that supplies energy not only to Mozambique but also to South Africa.

April 1974

The most exciting and hopeful news comes from Portugal. The so-called Carnation Revolution (*Revolução dos Cravos*)[1] has resulted in the overthrow of the dictatorship in Portugal. It seems that even the Portuguese are unhappy with how the government was managing the country and their colonies. What now for all the colonies and Portugal? I am excited to find out.

There is trouble emerging all over Africa and I certainly feel it in Mozambique, and, of course, I fully support their right to be independent. As for Timor, it is difficult to get regular news. We are hearing that political parties are forming in readiness to elect a Timorese Government. I wonder what I would do if I were there now.

June 1975

Being exiled was fate. Although it hurts to be separated from my country, I am grateful that my family is not caught up in the conflict between the political parties happening there

1 A peaceful military coup on 25 April 1974 that overthrew the Fascist dictatorship and ended Portuguese colonialism.

now. We could have so easily been caught up in the war that is tearing our communities apart. My heart aches as I hear news from Timor. Conflicts between the three major political parties are developing into fights in the streets and it is feared that a civil war could develop. This is not what I was expecting from my dear land and people. I hope that the political leaders can find some way out of all this despair. What is our future now? Will I ever be able to take my family back to our homeland?

I have managed to send money in a clandestine way to FRETILIN[2]. This group has also become a good source of news from my country. I even send money to some APODETI (political party that believed that Timor should integrate with Indonesia) members I had known when I became aware they were struggling in exile somewhere else.

August 1975

I am happy to hear that other Portuguese colonies are having a chance at becoming independent, too, but I am fearful of all the conflict being generated in all these countries.

September 1975

It seems that Fretilin has a chance of winning the civil war, but I am hearing disturbing news coming from the border with Indonesia. Could they be planning to invade my country? What chance do we have against an invading force if Portugal withdraws from Timor?

2 *Frente Revolucionária de Timor-Leste Independente* (The Revolutionary Front for an Independent East Timor): a resistance movement that fought for East Timorese independence from 1974, and formed the first government after Independence, with Xanana Gusmão appointed its inaugural president.

November 1975

Life goes on normally for us so far from home. Every day I go out and work to keep my family flourishing. Every month I keep reporting to the PIDE office to say I'm still here and working in Mozambique.

December 1975

The news from Timor is not good. The conflict between the three political parties continues to kill many innocent Timorese. The Portuguese are abandoning us at a very volatile moment in our history. Yes, we want independence, but Portugal, you cannot just withdraw when another country plans to invade; especially when for centuries, you have refused to train and educate us, to give us any chance to be anything.

Meanwhile, the people of Mozambique are celebrating their independence, and I am so glad to be here to witness such an auspicious occasion. If Frelimo (Mozambiquan Liberation Front) are able to overthrow the Portuguese, then I have complete faith in Fretilin being able to the same. The similarities in our causes—of freedom and liberation—are all too much alike. The way things are going, I'm sure Timor will be independent soon but I'm just really worried about Indonesian intentions.

December 1975

Devastating news: Timor declares independence for a few days, only to be invaded by Indonesia, as feared. We have no means of communication, no idea of what is happening to our families.

On the day of the invasion, I heard the news on the radio. I could not get any additional first-hand information as it was too dangerous for anyone to travel. We were despairing—not knowing if our family and friends were alive and safe, not knowing anything other than the complete horror we imagined.

The trouble has escalated in Mozambique, too. Mozambique's revolution is becoming dangerous. Now that they are independent, the local people are targeting the Portuguese and demanding that they all leave Mozambique. My family is again in danger, but once again my work saves me. The company I'm working for, *Atividades Eletricas e Associadas*, offers me a job in Portugal just as my house is raided by a Mozambiquan tribe. When they entered our house, it is obvious that they think that my wife is Portuguese, and because I'm working for a Portuguese/French company, they think that we pose a threat to the revolution. Luckily, our maids and cooks who were Mozambiquans, defended us and we were left unharmed but terrified.

I was not home at the time of the raid, but my wife and children were, and if our helpers had not intervened, I hate to think of the fate of our children. My wife recalls the cook standing in front of her, protecting her, and saying to the rebels, 'This family is good: this family has paid for my education, this family treats us with respect, this family is supporting many other families. You will not hurt this lady and their children; they are not our enemies.'

And so, our family was left untouched, but my wife grew very fearful as the news of Portuguese families disappearing became all too real. We decide it is no longer safe. I accept the offer in Portugal, and here we go again... We leave all my personal belongings to the maids and cook.

January 1976: Portugal

We arrived in Portugal safely and went to live with my sister, Otilia, in a small country town near the district of Coimbra. The Portuguese government had encouraged us to settle with the hordes of refugees coming from all the colonies, but we preferred to go where my sister was living. Otilda was married to a Portuguese man, whose family was from Redinha, the country town where we settled. We left Mozambique on a nice sunny day in summer and arrive in the freezing cold of a Portuguese winter. The shock to the family was not just cultural!

I continued to hear news from Timor via radio as well as from the steady influx of refugees. The war was devastating, horrific and there was still no news of our immediate family.

My new job took me to many different parts of the world some names of which I have forgotten! I spent time in Namibia, Angola, South Africa, Venezuela, Iraq and Israel. Because I was often away, and for long periods of time, I did not have the chance to participate in the flourishing Timorese community developing in the refugee camps surrounding Lisbon. The unexpected influx of refugees coming from all the troubled colonies claiming independence resulted in shanty towns developing on the outskirts of Lisbon which was where the majority of the Timorese settled.

Having a well-paid secure position on my arrival meant I was able to find a suitable house in the country town of Redinha to raise my children which, although not as luxurious as what we had in Mozambique, would do for now. At least there is no threat of any revolutions, and it is much better than what the Portuguese government is offering to the refugees in Balteiros refugee camp; the situation there is appalling. At least here in Redinha, there are lots of fields for our children to play soccer in and to make new friends. It was sad for my family to have left the friends we made in Mozambique, but I felt it was necessary to give my children the best opportunities and to raise them the very best way I can.

1976-1985

I am both relieved and happy to see my children fitting into this country and enjoying the luxuries Portugal has to offer. My boys are particularly skilful at soccer, a sport the Portuguese simply adore. Both have been offered contracts with the Sporting Club—the top soccer club in Portugal—which is quite promising at such a young age. My children have made many friends who will help them grow and flourish into good people. Although there are many differences between the cultures of the Timorese and the Portuguese, having one common language, the same religion and other customs, has resulted in my family's somewhat smooth transition to life in Portugal.

November 1976

Not one day goes by when I don't miss my country, my Timor. While I appreciate the countryside of Portugal, what I yearn for is to be able to wander off and smell the robust smell of our frangipani and coffee plants, and to behold the astounding sight of our true blanket of stars. Where I am now, tall industrial buildings obstruct my view. I live and I'm happy, my family is safe, secure and cheerful, but no matter what, a part of me will always be missing my homeland.

News arrives with each fresh group of refugees. Every day, more and more, all bringing terrible news of the brutal war Indonesia is raging in Timor while the rest of the world turns a blind eye to the atrocities my people are enduring. I can't imagine what horrible things can be happening to my friends and family, especially to those who are members of the Fretilin party.

My children are growing up in Portugal. I am extremely proud of them and how they have adapted to change. When I come back from work, I am always surprised to see them out and about, being curious and exploring with their friends, or relaxing and playing soccer. No matter how tough my day was, my children are always there to put a smile on my face.

The war in Timor still rages on. I try to put that aside every day, hoping for a letter that will tell me that Timor has become independent and the fighting settled, knowing very well that every letter we receive will contain sad news.

More and more Timorese are arriving, and now some are family. Most stay for a few years, only to move again, to re-settle in Australia. Portugal is not equipped to handle the refugee situation, so whenever possible, people are migrating to Australia. My wife and I are beginning to discuss the same move. We are not living in the shanty towns—and definitely would not want to—but it means we are very isolated from the rest of the Timorese community.

Finally, we received news from my wife's cousin who is offering to be our sponsor to migrate to Australia. Elizabete, my oldest daughter starts doing some research on that country: which town to settle in? We decided on Melbourne because of similar weather conditions to what we are now used to here, and the fact that my wife's family had already settled in there. The family was excited about our new journey. Here we go again…

July 1985: Australia

It has been eleven years, eleven years that I have both loved and hated—loved living in Portugal, but hated the fact that I left my true home, Timor-Leste. Once again we must move, but sadly, not to Timor. Staring at the empty plane seat in front of me, I could not consider this move as an opportunity, but as a betrayal of my country, my friends and my family still living there. As I turned around, I was hoping my children would cheer me up as they always did; instead I was faced with only blank faces. Even though we were excited about going to Australia, it was heartbreaking to be leaving many good friends.

July 1985

We leave sunny Portugal during a fine summer day, and arrive in Melbourne in what seems the coldest day we have ever experienced. It rained and rained and rained … with gloomy grey skies that seemed to never end.

On our arrival, we stayed in a very humble flat—small and cosy but just big enough for all of us. We were met by family and reunited with many close friends from back in Timor—friends I had not seen or heard of since 1971. It was good to be in Australia. I felt straightaway that I had made the right decision: I know this country is the land of opportunities.

Now we must adapt yet again, put the past behind us and live in the present. The independent, multicultural nature of Australia will be the best place for a permanent home that I can find.

Since there was a strong Timorese community in Melbourne, especially around the Endeavour Hills area, I soon became involved in the cultural and political scene, joining the Fretilin political party, very excited at finally being able to do something about the lost cause of the war in Timor. I chose to join Fretilin because it seemed to me that it was the only party that was doing the most relevant work in relation to the campaign for independence.

We worked hard at fundraising, sending money to the party as well as supporting other members of the Timorese community who were working abroad to promote the Timor-Leste cause. These included people such as Jose Ramos Horta, who was particularly active in the US, and other members scattered around the world, especially in Mozambique and Portugal.

We also dedicated ourselves to educating the Australian public about the situation in Timor; we needed to re-establish that friendship between Australians and Timorese that had been forged during the Japanese invasion. The Timorese supported the Australians then in 1942, and now it is Australia's turn to support the Timorese.

My life in Australia became a life of work, family, friends, and the struggle for my homeland. I participated in all the protests and cultural projects including plays, while continuing to send financial support via Fretilin.

In 1998 I had the privilege of travelling again to Europe, taking a photographic exhibition that drew parallels between the Holocaust and the East Timor situation. This was a collaboration between the Melbourne Jewish Museum and the Timorese community both here and in Ireland. The exhibition travelled to several countries, including Portugal, and gained a lot of public attention.

When in 1999, Indonesia was forced by the UN to hold a referendum in East Timor for the people to decide whether they wanted to have an independent country or be part of Indonesia, my heart nearly stopped. I went to Dandenong to vote, alongside my friends and family; it was beautiful to see the majority of the Melbourne Timorese community there.

Overwhelmingly, my people voted for independence! What a time to celebrate.

After so many years, Indonesia lifted the ban on travelling to Timor and, although I had been expelled from my own country never to be allowed to return (by the Portuguese authorities), I was overjoyed to know that now I could finally visit my true home.

In 2000, I was invited to go back to Timor to work in rebuilding the nation. I was elated to go back to my beloved *Timor Lorosa'e*[3] where, as a UN official, I worked as an electrician and mechanic. On arrival, however, I was not prepared for the devastation. After the Timorese people voted to be independent, the Indonesian military took their revenge, torching much of Dili and many other towns and villages, and decimating the surrounding countryside. It was devastating to see my house in Balide and my house in Bidau both burnt down, as were whole towns and streets including hospitals, schools, clinics, shops, and any house with links to Fretilin or Falintil[4].

---

3 'Timor' derives from 'timur', meaning 'east' in Malay; and 'Leste' also means 'east' in Portuguese; and 'Lorosa'e' means literally 'rising sun' in the East Timorese language of Tetum but is also used to indicate 'east'. So Timor-Leste or Timor Lorosa'e both mean 'east east'.

4 Armed wing of the pro-independence movement, the National Liberation of East Timor, founded in 1975.

But it was very humbling to meet people who still remembered me and my work, some of whom I had helped while I was working in the oil drilling company. However, I could see just how much work there was to do now, and I was not so young anymore.

When I had left Timor in the early 1970s, the nation was having trouble supplying electricity reliably and efficiently. Twenty-five years later, in 2000, here I am working on the same problem. This time, however, my expertise and experience are recognised. It is just so sad that the country has been left in such a dismal state. But I must stay positive… We are independent, after all.

20 May 2002

I am overjoyed to hear that my country's independence will be formally recognised worldwide. My daughters are coming from Melbourne to join me here in Timor for the independence celebrations. The whole country is in party mode; there are people from all over the world, and the Portuguese are proving to be amazing people, being so supportive of our new nation. We survived hundreds of years of colonisation and the most brutal of genocides, but now we are once again *Timor Lorosa'e*, Timor of the Rising Sun.

Australia is certainly home to me and my family and we are proud to be Australians, but we are equally proud to be Timorese. I can enjoy being part of both worlds and am at an age where I can watch and observe the development of both nations simultaneously. I think we still have a lot to learn from each other.

27 June 2016

I have decided that after all the hardships Timor has gone through, it's time to get *our* story known. We have met with some high school students who were happy to help. They have listened and written up our story. Our family story is to be published in a book. Now we will have my family's part in East Timor's story known. Yes, we shall get our story out there!

God bless all of you. Be honest and love each other, for ever and ever.

Now I have a few beliefs which I would like to share with you.

We must respect each other.

I'm not wise, but I have a lot of experience in life.

Ambition and power can consume someone.

You have to feel proud when you try to be what you want to be.

My country should be free—everyone should have a right to be free.

I would like to ask you, young people, when you grow up, please love each other… Everyone should be loved by everyone.

Everyone is part of one big family, and we all should support one another.

Carmelita Gomes

The three students who interviewed Carmelita for this project were moved to write her story in poetry form rather than prose.

Entering the new world
I was held in my mother's arms.
Her hands running through my curls
She'd kiss me on the cheek.

My home, my country, East Timor;
Your small land and diverse culture.
The people, the nature I adore,
Forever one proud community.

I remember my father once told me
That when you grow up on this earth,
You must love one another, don't you see?
He's a wise and curious man.

Like a book quote he would say:
'We all must listen to each other
And understand each other's ways'.
His words are always so encouraging.

He's a fighter, a determined being
And a man with many beliefs.
But who knew we would be fleeing
Suddenly from East Timor.

My home, my country, East Timor,
Your small land and diverse culture.
The people, the nature I adore;
Forever one proud community.

Our country deserves more.
Independence and freedom.
It shouldn't turn to war
Between our family and the government.

Timor to Mozambique,
We were exiled from our own country.
I was in a new place the next week,
Staying there till I was four.

Growing and learning as time went by,
Mozambique became our adopted home.
My family remembered waving goodbye
To their home, their country, East Timor.

Although only one year when we left,
No one likes to lose something precious,
Just like a mother torn from her son.
Will there ever be a day we go home?

My home, my country, East Timor,
Your small land and diverse culture.

The people, the nature I adore;
Forever one proud community.

I remember looking at the new night sky
In this hot tropical country;
It gave me a feeling to fly,
To dream and explore.

It was a chance to embrace
What Mozambique would offer.
To enjoy this new place,
Its culture and people.
Everything was all fine
In little Mozambique until
We had to leave quickly
And headed straight to Portugal.

We left due to their revolution,
And so, we moved again to a new country.
To me it was all confusion,
Just another adventure to journey.

I embraced life in the Portuguese countryside,
And made many new friends.
Dad visited so many exciting places,
And shared his wondrous adventures with us.

Oh, my country, East Timor, my real home.
What horror is happening to you?
How your people, my people, must be suffering.
When will it end? When can you be free?

Now I'm fifteen and Dad says best to move again.
This time to Australia, so far away from all I know.
So far away from all my friends.
I try hard to feel excitement but then it hits me!

Immense sadness begins to choke and overwhelm me,
Forcing tears to prickle behind my eyes.
The first time I'm old enough to understand
What being on a plane really represents.

This is not a big adventure anymore.
I'm not four years old now, I'm fifteen,
And this plane is leaving Portugal behind.
I'm leaving all I know and all I understand.

When I took my seat on the plane to Australia,
On 15 July 1985, thoughts of East Timor,
Memories of Mozambique and Portugal
Were flooding into my mind.
What now in Australia?

We have now arrived in Australia,
And I tell myself that I will make new friends soon,
And be able to return to sharing the things I love
with them.
Off to English classes tomorrow, so let's see!

Armed with a smile and a bag full of books
I was prepared for what would follow.
Crowds of people gave me strange looks,
I ignored them and walked straight ahead.

Upon arrival, I was filled with fear,
A worry that I wouldn't fit in.
It wasn't the most welcoming atmosphere,
I was afraid of others being mean.

A room full of people who felt the same as me?
We struggled to communicate,
But somehow together felt free.
It was our old memories that bonded us tight.

One look around the room, I tried to persevere,
I finally had a sense of belonging.
Everyone had their friends, but mine were not near,
They were all on the other side of the world.

I was a shy girl, isolated and afraid
When suddenly, a young girl approached me.
My feelings of loneliness started to fade
As she smiled and sat down beside me.

Our two worlds suddenly aligned,
As she and I became friends.
I didn't know someone could be so kind;
Two girls, one country, and some memories to make.

She'd always smile and be so bright.
Her personality always reminded me of home.
We'd talk all day, even at night,
When she came over or on the phone.

Upon arrival, I was filled with fear,
A worry that I wouldn't fit in.
Soon after, everything became clear
New school, new friends, new me.

Now, I am happy.

Written by Naomi Yong, Lily Lunder and Tome Correia, Gleneagles Secondary College, Melbourne, 2016.

Baptista Family

Pedro Baptista

My maternal grandfather, Jose Inacio Da Costa Mousinho, was born to Portuguese parents in Goa, which at the time, was a tiny coastal colony of Portugal, in British India. Following his schooling, he worked for the government there before transferring to a government position in Timor. At one time, grandfather had been the District Administrator of the Liquica District and was responsible for the building of the impressive administration and court buildings that remain there today. My grandmother, Ines De Jesus Nunes Mousinho, was from the Maubara District.

My mother, Maria Isabel, was the fourth born of eight children and grew up in the family house near the Dili waterfront about 300 metres from the Motael Church. Grandfather loved books and read widely; and had a reputation as an intellectual. As a student of the law and respected in the community, local people would come to him for advice, and he would often represent them in court.

During the Second World War, the Australian Special Forces were in East Timor prior to the Japanese forces invading. Many local people supported the Australian forces, but there were some Timorese called the *Coluna Negra* (Black Gang), who were informers for the Japanese army.

On one occasion, three Australian soldiers, fleeing from the Japanese, took refuge in the cellar under grandfather's house. When the Black Gang came with the Japanese soldiers looking for the Aussies, my grandfather was sick in bed. My grandmother tried unsuccessfully to communicate this to the Japanese soldiers, so grandfather wrote a note in English which was given to the soldiers that said, 'We haven't seen any Australians'. Fortunately for us and for the Australians, the Japanese went away, and the fugitives were able to escape.

Because grandfather refused to cooperate with the occupying Japanese, when he was ill and needed to go to hospital, proper care was not provided. As a consequence, he did not recover from his sickness and died in hospital.

It is estimated that during the Japanese occupation, 40,000 East Timorese died: the Portuguese in the concentration camps died from starvation, and the Timorese died from resisting the Japanese and helping the allies.

My mother was around 12 years old in 1942 when the Japanese occupied East Timor and remembers vividly the trauma the family experienced. She told me of one horrible experience: 'One dreadful day the Japanese soldiers ransacked our home, destroying most of my father's books. One soldier took one of my father's books and wiped his bum on it. Fortunately, some books were saved and were treasured by the family until 1975.' Sadly, during the intervening years under Indonesian rule when political instability prevailed and families were repeatedly dislocated or homes ransacked, the books were lost.

Mum also told me of the fate of another family member. 'My grandfather's brother, who lived in Liquica, had a radio and was able to listen to the news of the world. Someone informed on him and he was beaten to death by Japanese soldiers in front of his wife. She never recovered from this traumatic experience and died a few months later.'

All the Timorese living in Dili with some Portuguese background, were rounded up and forced to walk a very long distance to Boibau in the Ermera District where a concentration camp was set up. They slept in the bush on the way, and Mum remembered a friend being bitten by a scorpion, and the women using local herbal medicine to treat the bite.

Life in the camp was hard. They were on starvation rations, taking from the trees and plants whatever they could eat, boiling up whatever they couldn't manage to eat fresh. Mum told me that, 'Sometimes we were so desperate for food that we had to extract the tamarind pips from our poo and boil them up again. We also ate wild beans which are poisonous, so they had to be boiled up seven or eight times to extract the poison before they could be eaten safely. Tragically, my sister died in the camp from eating those wild beans.'

After the war, my mother, along with other teenage girls, was sent to the convent in Ermera Vila, where she boarded for her fifteenth and sixteenth years. She then started working as a nursing aide at the hospital in Dili and, at seventeen, she met and married my father, Antonio Pedro Baptista, and settled in Dili.

My father had been a Portuguese soldier who, during his compulsory military service in 1945 and 1946, had been posted to Mozambique and then East Timor. At the end of his military service and after the defeat of the Japanese, Antonio was invited to take up a government position in East Timor, in charge of a very remote regional post at Nitibe, in the enclave of Oecussi. It entailed him visiting Dili to provide regular reports, and it was on one of these visits that he met my mother. She seems to have been the incentive for him to transfer to Dili, where he got a job in the Department of Justice as a court recorder. Later, he was transferred to the Department of the Economy where he continued until he retired.

After the birth of her first five children, my mother trained as a nurse and practised at the same hospital where we were all born. Subsequently she was placed in charge of providing the blood transfusions in the operating theatre. I remember Mum being called out at night to attend emergency operations. Later, she trained as a midwife.

I have many treasured memories of a happy family living in comfortable conditions. My childhood seemed almost perfect, with lots of time spent outdoors going to the beach and us having many adventures. I realise that I was considered the rebel among the eleven children. I remember as a young teenager 'borrowing' my Dad's bike, his only mode of transport. A friend and I cycled to Liquica to attend the festival there. It was a 36-kilometre ride through the heat of the dry season. During that day while swimming at the local pool, I rescued a 10-year-old boy from drowning. We danced into the night and when the festival was over at 3 a.m. we, together with our bikes, were taken on a truck back to Dili. My Dad was tough but fair in his treatment of us, and on this occasion, I knew that he was disappointed with my behaviour. Both, Dad and Mum let me know that they were upset mainly because they didn't know where I was or if I was safe.

All the children in our family attended Portuguese government schools and followed the Portuguese curriculum. I remember school as a happy time with lots of friends. Each morning before school, I have fond memories of our house filled with conversations accompanied by the aroma of brewing coffee made from beans that had come from my grandmother's coffee plantation in Maubara. After school each day, we had to do our homework and daily chores before going outside for another game of soccer, a swim or a sail at the beach, until darkness brought us back home for the evening meal.

In the early years of high school, I was more interested in the outdoors than the classroom which was reflected in my results; they were certainly not as good as my parents thought they should be. My Dad's response was, 'If you are not going to settle to study then you need to experience the alternative—real work'.

So, he arranged for me, at the age of 15, to spend all my school holidays working for a company that handled car parts. My boss was Mr Amandio Gomes who was a friend of my father's and, though he was a fair boss, he also made me work very hard. Dressed in shorts and thongs I did whatever manual labour needed to be done. All day I carried car parts from one place to another.

On one occasion I dropped a heavy car part on my foot and another time I stood on a nail. While I received the necessary medical attention from my mother, there was still the expectation that I would go straight back to work after being patched up.

At the end of my time there, I had missed out on my fun-filled school holidays but at least I earnt some money—

enough to buy a second-hand bike. Now I didn't need to 'borrow' my Dad's bike if I was silly enough to be tempted! Looking back on my three months of work experience, I do agree that my wise, 'tough' father taught me a valuable lesson.

My Mum wanted me to study medicine, and by the time I was in my final years of *Liceu* (high school), I was committed to further study and was hoping to go to Portugal to attend medical school. My father had retired at the age of 55, and planned to buy a coffee plantation in Maubara. But unfortunately, these plans were interrupted by political changes in Portugal which then began to affect the lives of my family and the lives of everyone in our East Timor.

Following the military coup in Portugal in April 1974 that was initiated by some captains of the Portuguese army, the new Portuguese leaders wanted to withdraw from all their colonies. The Portuguese Minister for Foreign Affairs, Almeida Santos, stated that, 'The colony of East Timor is like a cruise ship in the Pacific Ocean. It is hugely expensive, everyone on board is having a good time, and nothing of value is being produced.' He went on to say that it was a popular place for Portuguese public servants to be posted, where they enjoyed a relaxed lifestyle and could live economically, and where they received a Government allowance on top of their salary.

Decolonisation began with the Portuguese Governor encouraging local people to establish political parties. Three main political parties had formed: Fretilin, UDT (Timorese Democratic Union) and Apodeti. Fretilin and UDT both wanted independence from Portugal but differed greatly in how and when this should be achieved. Fretilin party members wanted independence immediately and were encouraged by three visiting Portuguese army officers with the rank of major, who had been sent to East Timor to assess the situation and encourage independence as soon as possible. UDT party members wanted independence staged over a ten-year period. Apodeti was in favour of integration with Indonesia. All three parties ran information sessions in Dili and throughout the districts.

In March and April 1975, Fretilin party members began demonstrating, holding information sessions where they shouted aggressive slogans: Get rid of the Portuguese, Timor for the Timorese and similar. Those of us whose families were UDT supporters began to feel unsafe, convinced that Fretilin supporters were coming after us; at night, we always walked in groups of five or six for protection. I became an active member of Lesvalt, the youth wing of UDT. Some of my friends at school were Fretilin supporters, so by day we talked, but at night, we were potential enemies.

The political conflicts started to impact on my schooling. I remember one day a fight breaking out when a mob of angry workers from a nearby SAPT (*Sociadede Agricola Patria Trabalho*) coffee processing plant barged into our school armed with sticks and traditional spears. These men were Fretilin supporters from the eastern districts, and would have identified our school as having mostly students with a Portuguese background, and therefore more likely to be UDT supporters. Things were about to get bloody when the police intervened. Everyone was caught up in the political conflict.

Leaders from the three political parties also visited neighbouring countries to elaborate on their policies. My uncle, who was vice president of the UDT Party, was one of the officials who travelled to Indonesia. They were told very clearly by Indonesian officials that, 'President Suharto would not tolerate in their region an independent country with a socialist regime'.

Increasingly during1975, living and working in Dili became very difficult. My father, himself a UDT supporter, had had a lifetime friendship with Xavier Do Amaral, the president of the Fretilin Party, who was the godfather of my older brother, Almerindo. At one stage, Xavier warned my father that the political conflict was going to deteriorate and advised him to take his large family away from Dili, and maybe even, far away to Portugal. UDT leaders also warned my father of the dangers his family could face if they stayed in the capital. This was enough to convince my father who wasted no time gathering up all the family documents in preparation for us to leave the country; hopefully, to return when the political situation was more stable.

On the morning of the day of our departure, Mum, Dad, my two sisters and two of my brothers flew from Dili to Baucau. As I was waving off my family at the Dili airport, I saw Fretilin supporters making notes of the families who were leaving. Among them were two I knew well: Antonio Pinheiro, who had been a good friend since Grade 2, and the 16-year-old brother of Nicolau Lobato who was to become the first Prime Minister of an independent East Timor for the few days between the Portuguese authorities withdrawing and the Indonesian invasion in December 1975. Since the developing political tensions through 1974, Antonio had become abusive towards me saying, 'You are Portuguese! Go back to Portugal.'

In the evening of that same day, the rest of we boys—my five brothers and I—travelled to Baucau by barge. My sister Emilia and her husband Xanana Gusmão and their two children, were there to see us off. With sadness in our hearts, we waved goodbye knowing that we may never see them again.

We shared the barge with other fleeing families and Portuguese soldiers who were returning to Portugal at the end of their tour of duty. Travelling on the open ocean, the waves were at times huge and the smell of diesel was almost overpowering. I recall some young Portuguese soldiers crying for their mothers as the barge went through the waves. My brothers and I had spent our early lives by the sea, swimming and sailing, so we were not in the least worried by the rough journey.

When we arrived next morning in Baucau, my uncle had arranged for a car to take us to the Posada Baucau—the impressive hotel he managed—where we had a delicious breakfast before being taken at midday to the Baucau Airport. It was 12 May 1975 when we boarded a Portuguese Airforce plane and flew out to Portugal.

My family soon settled into life in Portugal in Alviobeira, a small village 10 kilometres from the city of Tomar, a beautiful place where my father's family had originally come from. We rented a house on a very large piece of land owned by an old lady who lived on the property. There was a well about 50 metres from our house, but when my father asked if he could lay a water pipe to our home as she had done to hers, she refused. As a consequence, our family's daily routine included a one-kilometre walk to and from the community well, pulling a handcart containing ten 20-litre plastic containers of water. Rain, hail, or shine, we would use the hand pump at the well to haul up the water each day; in the summer we would usually have to collect water twice each day. At times the collection was the subject of some arguments among the members of the family when younger children, who did not have water collection as their responsibility, used what their older siblings considered was more water than they should.

Fortunately, my father had a small piece of land about a kilometre away with its own well which had been passed to him by his parents. This is where we grew our vegetables and fruit all year round because we were able to irrigate it. Unused land adjacent to our block was offered to us also to extend our productive garden.

I have vivid memories of harvesting the potatoes during the summer school holidays. Using a special tool designed so the potatoes would not be damaged, the older kids had to dig the very hard, sun-baked soil, and as the potatoes were uncovered, the younger ones would gather them up and bag them. We were particularly careful not to damage any of the potatoes as Dad would be very upset. They were spread out in the loft and Dad would cover them with a white powder which prevented moth infestation; this way they would keep for many months.

Another fond memory from this time was olive harvesting in November when the whole family worked together as a team. Since it was a very cold time of the year in our village, we would build a fire close by to keep warm, then spread nets under the trees and using our bare hands, strip the olives down onto the nets. At lunchtime we stopped to eat the bread and meat we had brought from home.

On reflection, I realise that the very physical life we led during our teenage years in Portugal made our bodies strong and fit which prepared us for the manual labouring jobs we had to do in Portugal, and later, when we arrived in Australia.

We made the most of our life in Alviobeira and as a family with 10 teenagers, we certainly made an impact. Within three weeks, my Dad offered to organise his children to play music in the main street on a Saturday night. I remember my brothers, Almerindo, Mario and Cesar, playing accordions while the rest of us all danced to the Portuguese music. During the evening the hat was handed round to collect for the musicians, my brothers. These street parties, with sometimes up to 200 attending, became a regular happening and were loved by the local people, particularly the young people.

Many years later, in 2015 when I returned to Alviobeira, people told me what a big improvement our family had made to 'the entertainment' of their village over the nine years of our stay; and how we were missed when we left.

Not everyone in the village welcomed us, however. Some of the older people were suspicious of this large family from Timor, sometimes blaming us for things we did not do. When chickens were stolen, they said, 'These Timorese come here and steal our chickens'. We were blamed, too, when a street sign was broken. Another time, we were with some friends from the village at a small lake and noticed a fire up in the mountains. Next thing, a local man arrived and pointing a gun at us, accused us of starting the fire, whereupon he proceeded to call the police.

I completed high school successfully and was looking forward to studying medicine. Dad was still contemplating returning to a coffee plantation in Maubara once the conflict in our country was resolved. Mum being the dedicated professional she was, had resumed working as a nurse and midwife as soon as we were settled in Portugal. She worked in two clinics and a hospital, going from one to the other as the need arose, not taking a day's leave for the next nine years.

Following high school and before starting university, my girlfriend and I were married and our baby son, Pedro Junior, was born. With this added responsibility, I had to give up my plans to study medicine and instead, work to support my own family. My first job was at a company which bought and distributed wine. Later on, I had a good and well-paid job in a paper-making factory in Aveiro city, working in the maintenance team that built scaffolding inside and outside silos—similar to wheat silos—where the paper pulp was stored. I now realise that this was a dangerous job and we didn't ever use harnesses—occupational health and safety hadn't yet arrived on the sites where we were working.

My brothers also earnt their living doing a range of dangerous jobs. Cesar was working with bricklayers and digging wells. In the latter job, a large bucket, the size of half a 44-gallon drum, was lowered down to the men digging the well which they filled with the soil and rocks, before it was winched up again. If the winch mechanism had failed, there would have been casualties.

Conscripted to serve in the army for two years, and selected for the Special Forces Commando Regiment—the Red Berets—I recollect that the training was intense, but taking part in NATO military exercises was a highlight for a young man. At the end of the compulsory two years which all young Portuguese men had to complete, I was offered the opportunity to attend the military college to become an officer and make the army my career. I was also offered another opportunity, to become a mercenary, fighting in Africa—both highly paid and dangerous. It was during this time, when Pedro Junior was only two, that my wife and I decided to end our marriage and share the custody of Pedro Junior.

So at the end of my national service, I left the army and began working on building sites, doing long days, and sleeping in sheds where we cooked our own meals. On one job, I had worked for nearly one month but had not been paid, so I travelled to the city of Leiria to meet the owner of the construction company and ask for my pay. He demanded that I get out of his office, but I stood my ground, and my pay arrived two weeks later. I know for sure that if I had not made a stand I would not have been paid; and I needed that money to survive.

My lifelong dream had always been to live in Australia. As a boy of seven years old, I had the opportunity to watch a documentary on life in Australia which promoted a prosperous and happy life 'down under'. I remember the image of Australian school students in neat school uniforms, eating apples; and it also showed amazing sea turtles swimming in the ocean.

So, that's what I did in 1984. I arrived on Australian shores with a little suitcase, $40 and big dreams! My father had given me $60 to take to Australia, but on the way we stopped at Singapore where I spent $20 on an amazing watch with all electronic gadgets including a calculator. When I finally arrived in Sydney I celebrated with my brother, Almerindo—who, together with his wife and son, had migrated a year earlier—by spending another $20 on a slab of VB beer. I had $20 left to start my life in my new country.

Sponsored under the Family Reunion Program by my Auntie Guida Lopes who was already living in Australia, I had also successfully applied to a Catholic Organisation in Lisbon, which financed my fare on the condition that I pay it back once I started working. Fortunately, my auntie welcomed me into her home even though my brother and his family were already living with her.

Soon after, we moved into a flat in Homebush together and I was helped by unemployment benefits for a couple of months until I found a job. We managed with weekly visits to the Flemington Market where we were often able to negotiate a five-dollar purchase of a large box of leftover fruit and vegetables.

My first job took me to Canberra where I linked up with a friend from East Timor and we worked making concrete lids for pits and curbing. Physically, this was a very demanding job as we had to lift the steel formwork filled with wet concrete off the benches, to be stored to set. It was winter, so we were freezing and sometimes the water froze; but life was good. Each Friday afternoon we caught the bus to Sydney to meet up with my brother and the family. After a wonderful weekend of parties with Timorese and Australian friends, on Sunday evening we would catch the bus back to Canberra ready for work the next day.

While living in Canberra, I met David Martins, another Timorese who was also a distant relative. He encouraged me to move to Melbourne and offered me a place to stay in Coburg. So in July 1984 I headed south, hoping to find a better job. I moved in with my cousins who were renting a house in Westall, in the south-east, and got a job at Silcraft making parts for cars.

The following year, I gained custody of my son who had been living mainly with my parents in Portugal and was fortunately able to arrange for my parents and Pedro Junior to join me in Australia. This was in a time when the Australian government accepted family reunions for people to migrate if they already had close family living here.

When they arrived in August 1986, Pedro Junior was seven years old. My parents settled in Melbourne's south-east, first in Westall and later, in Dandenong. They were very keen to learn English so enrolled in English Language classes at the nearby Enterprise Migrant Hostel. There were other Timorese families in the class, most of whom were living in the hostel.

Unfortunately, during the first class a significant setback happened. The teacher used some Indonesian expressions which confirmed to the Timorese their suspicions that she was, in fact, Indonesian. At the end of the lesson my father reportedly said: 'They (the Indonesians) have invaded our country, they have taken our land and they have killed our people. Now they have come here to teach us English? No!

This will not happen!' My father's emotional outburst had an immediate effect: the teacher was replaced, and their English classes continued.

❖❖❖

My amazing and indefatigable Mum enrolled at RMIT for a one-year course to gain Australian nursing qualifications. At the end of the year she worked at Monash Medical Centre and later, at a nursing home in Noble Park.

My father had been highly regarded throughout Timor, particularly in Bazartete and Maubara. He had helped the local people fight to retain their land when the authorities wanted to change the boundaries between districts. When I visited Bazartete in 2002, my father's godson, Domingos Baptista, told me that, 'Because of your father's support and skill, the families here were able to keep their land'. I was very proud, and grateful.

This poem reflects on the thoughts and emotions of a young Pedro Baptista as the effects of the civil war force him to make a life-changing decision.

Disaster stretched before my very eyes,
Politics causing the peaceful and happy place I called home to be unsafe.
The future everyone wanted is on the verge of destruction.
Fights between rival political parties carried out on the streets.
Friends from my childhood becoming enemies by night.
We are afraid to go out on our own.

Trying my best to ignore what is happening I solemnly walk to my favourite refuge
...the beach.
The sand is warm beneath my feet and the cool evening air tickles, blowing away all my worries.
The water softly rolls onto the shore, washing away my anxiety and nervousness.

Reality! Sounds of angry people, reminding me of how life is right now,
Memories swim all around me, as if I am drowning in water, forgetting how
To swim in the ocean, full of the memories. The beautiful scene around me turns into my worst nightmare,
The future of East Timor, about to be destroyed.
What now? The thought sinking into my head.

What now? This one question leaving me baffled
and terrified.
What now? This one question leaves me on the
brink of breaking down.
The decision has to be made…

I run home, keeping low, afraid to be seen by my
new enemies.
I now know that I must join with my family and
leave our country.
My family is the most important thing to me, yet my
heart is aching for my country.
East Timor is my home; is where my heart, soul and
body will always be.

It is time, I think, as sweat drips from my face,
soaking my shirt as I run back home.
The decision is harsh and the thought of what I
must do will leave me broken.
I have to do it, 'And I will', I whisper to myself, in
between short, wheezy breaths.
It is time to leave East Timor.

Written by Nikitha Ramkumar, Gleneagles Secondary College, Melbourne 2016.

Emilia's Story

My sister Emilia, whom I last saw at the Dili Port in May 1975, told me her story many years later.

When the Indonesians invaded in December 1975, all the men who supported Fretilin, including Emilia's husband, Xanana Gusmão, fled to Alieu. Emilia and her son Nito, and daughter Zeni, continued to live in a small house in Farol in Dili, and she continued working in the finance section of the Education Department. So Emilia had to raise her children alone as Xanana was in the jungle with the guerrilla fighters and would have been unable to visit his family.

When Xanana took over the leadership of the Timorese resistance force, Falintil, in 1981, the lives of Emilia and her children suddenly changed dramatically for the worse. Being the wife of the leader of the resistance, she became a target for those Indonesian army and security forces that wanted to crush any resistance to their occupation of East Timor. She was taken away day or night to be interrogated for hours on end as they tried to get information on the movements of her husband. Carted off at short or no notice, Emilia had to leave her children with neighbours and friends.

Despite the regular interrogations, as well as the threats and rocks being thrown on her roof, Emilia and her two children stayed in Dili. During this time, my parents managed to maintain phone contact with her as my Auntie Carolina had continued managing the Hotel Turismo in Dili, so would arrange for Emilia to be in the hotel when her parents phoned from Australia. Aware that the Indonesian authorities would be monitoring their calls, Emilia had to be very guarded in her conversation.

I was extremely worried about her and wanted to visit, but she would not agree to me coming up as she said that it was too dangerous for me, and there would be repercussions for her children and for herself afterwards. Emilia said to me, 'As the brother-in-law of Xanana, you might be taken away or maybe disappeared forever'. Eventually, working through the International Red Cross, in 1990 my parents managed to sponsor Emilia and the children out to Australia where they stayed for the next ten years.

Two years later, Emilia's husband was captured and taken to jail in Jakarta. Again, through the International Red Cross, I arranged for Emilia and the children to visit him there on two occasions. After the history-making referendum vote for independence in 1999, Emila decided to move to Darwin to be closer to Timor. A year later, with the Indonesians safely out of East Timor, Emilia took her children back home to live permanently in the same little house in Dili where she lives today. Both her children have built businesses there.

When I reflect on my life and where I now belong, I see myself as an Australian. My dream to settle in Australia has come true. On 24 September 1987 at the Oakleigh Mechanics Institute, I became an Australia citizen. My partner, Irene, and I had two daughters, Janine in 1991 and Alana in 1998. My brothers and sisters, excepting Emilia, are all here in Australia. The saddest moment of my life was in September 2014 with the unexpected death of my daughter, Janine, at the very young age of 23.

◈◈◈

My heritage is Portuguese and Timorese. I see Portugal as a place for holidays where I enjoy the company of family and friends, the amazing food and the beautiful city of Tomar. I love returning to Timor-Leste to see Emilia and all my extended family. And I love the countryside where I can relive many happy memories of my childhood. I continue in whatever way I can to assist in the development of this new nation. Maybe when I retire I will spend several months each year in Timor helping on the ground, passing on the skills that I have developed in my adopted country, maybe establishing a business.

Boavida Family

MEIRELES BOAVIDA

My paternal grandfather Jose Qui-Tunga, was from Mozambique, a Portuguese colony, and served in the Portuguese army. He had a wife and four children in Mozambique when he was transferred to serve in East Timor sometime in the 1920s. He spent the rest of his life in Timor and never saw his Mozambique family again.

He met my grandmother Cai-Dau, a Timorese girl from Bobonaro and when he retired from the army, he joined the Police Force there. My grandparents bought a large piece of land in Taibessi, which is now a suburb of Dili, where they were able to grow fruit and vegetables and keep chickens and pigs. They would have been living a comparatively comfortable life.

My Dad, Henrique, was born in 1934, the fourth child of Jose and Cai-Dau. By the time the Japanese and Australian forces came to Timor in 1942 there were six children in the family and they were living in Dili. We know from stories our parents have told us that life during the Japanese occupation was very hard for our family. Dad was about eight when the family fled for their lives, initially east towards Manatutu. They continued to move around for the three years until the end of the war, planting vegetables where they could for food, while trying to hide from the Japanese. One of our uncles worked with the Australian forces but that was considered very dangerous. We were told that approximately 40,000 Timorese were killed by the Japanese, and most for helping the Australians.

After the end of the war, my grandparents moved the family back to Taibesse where the children attended school and learnt to read and write in Portuguese. Dad told us that life immediately after the war, when he was about 11 years, was actually harder than it had been before. Some years later when the children were older, Grandfather divided his land among his family, and our father received a piece about as big as two house blocks. After leaving school, Dad went to work with one of his uncles and learnt how to be a mechanic. But he'd always aspired to be a nurse, so initially he worked in a clinic as a volunteer to show his commitment and his good attitude. From then on, nursing was to be our Dad's job and his love for the rest of his working life.

In the 1950s, Dad met and married Filomena, a Timorese girl from Ainaro who was living with her sister in Dili, but had spent all her young life in a remote village and had not had the opportunity to go to school.

All nurse training was on the job. So when Dad had demonstrated he was sufficiently skilled and worthy of a paid position, he was sent to a clinic in a small village called Cai-Laco, in the Ermera District. This was before any of we children were born.

When they needed medical supplies, they had to be fetched from Dili, which they did on horseback. One day, Dad and his brother-in-law, were crossing the river Loes on their way back from Dili loaded with supplies when they were attacked by robbers. Tragically, Dad's brother-in-law was killed, but my father managed to hide and then escape.

After a few years, my parents returned to Dili where Dad was able to take up his studies once again. They had already begun their family with the birth of Mario, Ligia, and Maria. In fourth place, I was born in Dili in 1962. Mum and Dad worked hard, growing fruit and vegetables and keeping chickens and other animals on their piece of land in Taibesse. As we grew older we were each given jobs to do to help Mum in the garden, using handmade tools to dig out weeds or turn the soil over ready to plant the corn and other crops before the wet season began.

My Dad loved his work and was very keen to learn as much as he could. I remember him studying from notes he had taken while at the hospital observing and listening to the nurses in charge. Each day he would return home at 5 p.m., eat some food and immediately begin his study while we children all played outside.

Dad received his first promotion to the town of Aileu where the clinic was based. With an assistant, he would travel on horseback to all the surrounding small villages. Sometimes they were away from home for four days and nights attending to the health needs of the people and delivering the vaccination programs.

They provided the only health service available to the people of the Alieu District; my father was considered to be the doctor and the nurse. As a consequence, he was well-liked and respected throughout the district. If there was an emergency requiring specialist treatment only available in

Dili, then an ambulance was called. My father's brother was an ambulance driver and I can remember him coming to Alieu to collect very ill patients. Dad's next promotion took us back to Dili, and Dad to the Dili Hospital where he rose to become the Head of Nursing, remaining in that position until the civil war.

With the increase in his salary, Dad was able to lease some land in Hera where we grew rice. Even though there were now nine children plus one additional adopted son, my parents provided us with a happy life, plenty of good healthy food and a school to attend. We felt safe and secure.

We were brought up to respect those in authority and to acknowledge that the rule of Portugal was the rule of Timor; we just accepted that we lived in a part of Portugal. We honoured the Portuguese flag and when it flew, we were taught to never step on its shadow. I remember the special flag-raising ceremony at 8 a.m. each Sunday or public holiday at the *Palacio de Reparticao*[5] in Dili. A trumpeter would play the Portuguese anthem and we would all stand to attention as the flag was raised. At 5 o'clock, before sunset, it was lowered again.

When I was nine years old, my older sister, Maria, and I were sent to boarding schools in Ossu, but Maria's convent school was some distance from my own which was beside the church. Portuguese was the only language allowed to be spoken there, and if we were heard speaking Tetum or any local dialect, we were punished. We were also punished if we couldn't answer questions or if we made mistakes with our

5 This grand building housed the colonial administration offices and since independence, it is used for government offices.

school work. After dinner, those to be punished for that day would have to come forward, put out their hand and receive a hit from a knotted strap. I still remember how much it hurt; all we could do was crawl under our blanket at night and wish that we were home with our Mum and Dad.

On Sundays the girls, guarded by the nuns, marched down to church and were seated on one side of the church while we boys sat on the other. Maria and I would steal a look at each other and as our eyes met, we connected and felt some happiness. I stayed at the boarding school for three years, returning home each summer holidays. At the age of 12, I entered the seminary in Dare to study to become a priest but decided against that vocation and returned home to my family.

Living in Dili meant that we could receive news of international events. The Portuguese government radio station provided daily news each evening and it broadcast all day Sunday. So at the age of 12, I remember my parents and their friends discussing the April 1974 Carnation Revolution coup in Portugal and the downfall of the regime. One of my cousins, Carvarino (Mau-Liar) who had been studying in Portugal, returned to Dili promoting the philosophy of the new leaders of Portugal: that East Timor should no longer be a colony of Portugal and should become an independent country.

Over the second half of 1974 it became clear that Portugal did really intend to withdraw from Timor as soon as possible. In anticipation of a new political structure to replace Portuguese rule, a number of groups, reflecting future options, founded three main political parties: Fretilin,

UDT or Apodeti. As people joined one of the three parties, tensions developed within families, friendships were tested, and splits occurred within communities. These tensions were even present in my family where Dad joined and worked for the more moderate UDT party and his eldest son, Mario, became a member of the radical Fretilin party. I remember the noisy demonstrations that were held in the streets and knew that my brother Mario was part of those.

Eventually, however, Mario respected Dad's authority and when the political situation deteriorated, he stayed with his family. This was not the case with other families we knew. My cousin, Carvarino, remained a Fretilin supporter and died in the resistance fighting during the later Indonesian invasion.

In August 1975, as the political situation got worse, the Portuguese army officials and civil authorities took refuge on Atauru Island, a three-hour boat trip away. There were still some Portuguese soldiers left at the army headquarters, however, and when the UDT forces attempted to take it over, we could hear the gunshots, as our house in Taibessi was just behind the base. We were told that one Timorese soldier in the Portuguese army who was on guard duty at the time, was shot in the failed attempt. The next day UDT set up a temporary headquarters behind the Motael Church in Farol and from there took over control of Dili.

At this point, we were told by reliable sources that our family was in immediate danger and it was no longer safe for us to live in Taibesse. Mario, Uncle Artur and I went with Dad to the UDT headquarters where Dad demanded a truck and back-up forces. Mario and Dad then drove back to our house to pick up Mum, Maria, Ligia and the younger kids. When Dad's nephew, who was a Fretilin member, tried to stop the truck from leaving, Dad pointed a gun at him and shouted, 'Nephew, don't!', and drove on. To Uncle Artur and me anxiously waiting at UDT headquarters, it seemed to take forever for our family to arrive, although it was probably less than an hour before we were all reunited.

The UDT headquarters behind the Motael Church became the base for its members and their supporters in Dili. Tents were set up on every spare plot and a large kitchen hall established to supply all our meals. Our family was allocated one tent about the size of a small living area in an Australian home. Mum, Dad, Uncle Artur and our 11 kids all squashed in together, sleeping on thin mats. It was uncomfortable but having all our family together in one tight space did provide us with a feeling of security.

The UDT forces set aside a big room for captured Fretilin supporters, one of whom was my cousin, Domingos. Others among the Fretilin prisoners were well-known to my parents, some of whom had been patients of Dad. I remember Mum smuggling food to Domingos at one time. Tragically, as invariably happens in these inflamed situations, he and another Fretilin supporter were shot while being detained; we were told that they had tried to escape, but I don't know whether that was the truth. His death at the UDT camp where we were sheltering, created a division and hatred in our family that was never to heal.

Within a few weeks, Fretilin forces regrouped and began taking over control of Dili which meant that all UDT supporters had to flee the city. Our family fled, this time on foot along the road to Liquica. As we walked, Mum was in front and Dad was behind, urging us to hurry for our lives. We stayed in Liquica for one week then had to flee again from the advancing Fretilin forces towards Maubara, where a UDT-organised truck arrived to take us into Vatuvo.

After a few weeks, we were on the run again. This time we headed for Atabae on the Timorese coast near the border with Indonesia. But even here, we had to continue walking as Fretilin forces were also in that area. We arrived in Mota-Ain, at the mouth of the river on the coast where we were able to stay for two weeks. I remember swimming in the sea and seeing Indonesian soldiers for the first time ever.

One Sunday morning, war caught up with us yet again, as we were bombarded by Fretilin forces. Many of our group died, and others were badly wounded; I still have vivid memories of the horrific injuries. Once again on foot, our family of Mum, Dad and 11 kids fled for our lives: Mum remained in front, Dad at the back, with Mario, the eldest, helping the little ones where he could. This time there were mortar shells landing all around us. On the way, Dad and two or three other nurses had to act as surgeons in makeshift hospitals, attending to horrific wounds caused by these shells.

When we finally reached the border, the Indonesian authorities let us pass through without trouble, and we kept walking on into the night. Next day, Indonesian army trucks arrived and took us on to Atambua where many other Timorese were already sheltering. For the next two weeks we were allowed to sleep in the S.D.Tiga primary school building at night but had to leave during the day with all our possessions, so the local Indonesian kids could attend their classes. A large portable shed was quickly erected to house all the families into what became our permanent shelter. There were no internal partitions or furniture, so adults set about making beds and providing privacy. Gradually families began planting vegetables and sharing their produce.

While there, we were very fortunate to reconnect with Francis, a family member whose parents had taken them all to live in Indonesia many years earlier. He was able to help us understand the language and took us to meet his family; we were able to trade some of our meagre possessions with them for food and other necessities. An Indonesian government school was established in the camp and it was compulsory for all the children to begin to learn how to speak and write the Bahasa language. We continued life in the camp for more than a year.

The UDT leaders had brought 23 Portuguese army officers with them to Atambua, and Portugal was keen for them to be returned to Portugal. It appears that those army officers were used as a bargaining tool by the UDT officials to guarantee the passage to Portugal of my family and the many, many more Timorese who had fled across the border. During August 1976, we travelled in an Indonesian government truck to Atapupo on the coast and boarded a small boat that took us to a large Indonesian army ship bound for Denpasar. From there we were flown to Honolulu where we spent an amazing day before flying on to Portugal. I well remember seeing US police officers wearing pistols on their hips and large cowboy hats on their heads just like the characters in all the Westerns we had seen in the cinema back in Dili.

It was 26 August 1976 and I was 13 years old when we arrived in Lisbon after this long journey. Mum, who was pregnant, and several of my brothers and sisters who had suffered sea and air sickness, were taken straight to hospital for treatment.

We settled into army tents at the refugee camp, Balteiros, which was also the home of refugees arriving from all the former Portuguese colonies including Angola and Mozambique. People of Portuguese background from each of these places were escaping the conflicts in their respective countries following the unplanned withdrawal of Portuguese rule. We were well looked after, with three meals a day provided; and when the school year began in October, we were allocated public transport vouchers to take us to school. Once again Portuguese was the language used in our classrooms and we had returned to the Portuguese curriculum that we had followed in Timor. Our brief introduction to the Indonesian language while spending the year in Atambua soon became a faint memory.

Our mother, Filomena, who was pregnant with her twelfth child at the time of our journey from the Indonesian refugee camp in Atambua to the Balteiros refugee camp in Portugal, died three months later while giving birth to her baby boy. After surviving so much, it was utterly devastating for us all! When I think back, poor Dad had lost his wife and companion who was his partner through so many dangerous situations as they brought their large family to safety.

There must have been little time for him to grieve, though, as baby, Filomeno, needed to be cared for as well as 11 other children to support and provide for. I remember my older sister Maria, taking responsibility for the cooking and caring for the baby while continuing on with her schooling. My older brother Mario, also tried to assist Dad by finding himself a job to help our family finances. The older children comforted the younger ones; and somehow, we all got through the next few days and the months that followed.

Balteiros became our home and our community for more than ten years. When Dad resumed his work as a nurse, we children took on more responsibility for looking after ourselves. Life was full and interesting. We enjoyed meeting refugees from the many other cultures, especially those from Mozambique with whom we felt we shared a common bond knowing that this was where our paternal grandfather, Jose Qui-Tunga, had come from. Soccer was the game we all loved, whichever culture we were from. Teams were formed in the camp and soccer tournaments were one of the highlights.

Venues were available for clubs to use and a Timorese club which we called Kablake (a mountain in East Timor) was established. Our club's activities included soccer, basketball, athletics, table tennis and East Timorese culture. The culture group had as its purpose the preservation of the Timorese culture to ensure it would be passed on to the younger members of the community.

A group of Timorese friends and my brother Elvis, my girlfriend Sandra, and I, got together to play Timorese music. We were soon performing in the camp, then decided to take our music beyond the camp. This was sufficient incentive for us to practise, learn quickly and improve. We named our group KDADALAK which in Tetum means 'streams joining together'. Symbolically the name of our group was saying that when we join together we become stronger.

We began learning from the elders and teaching our younger compatriots the Tebe dancing, (traditional Timorese dancing) and the traditional songs, our group ranging in age from six to 50 years old. We really enjoyed demonstrating our dances and sharing our music with other cultures in the camp, but it wasn't long before we were invited to perform in other venues. And so, we began to travel throughout Portugal. It was at this stage that we realised how much we wanted to retain and celebrate our Timorese culture, and that we actually had a responsibility to do so.

After our Portugal tour, we received invitations to perform in Spain and France. We all embraced this opportunity to share our culture and to say, 'the Timorese should have the same opportunity to be free like you'. I remember in Spain, how emotional I became when I recited the poem, 'Bury my heart in Mount Ramelau', by Timorese poet Borges da Costa.

In hindsight I realise that there were three vital aspects of the Timorese fight for independence. One was the Falantil, the Timorese heroes fighting the Indonesian army in Timor. The second was the international campaign raising awareness of the distressed state of the Timorese people, led by politicians and activists such as Jose Ramos Horta. The third was the celebration and sharing of a culture by a proud people who were insisting that their culture should be retained. I am proud to say that our cultural group, formed in the Balteiros camp, played an important part in the fight for an independent East Timor.

After three years in Portugal, at the age of 16, I began working as a labourer on building sites during the school holidays. It was good to be able to earn some money for myself and to assist Dad with the family finances. When school was to resume I decided to work full-time and attend classes at night, which I managed to do for one year by attending the Liceu D. Joao De Castro where I studied Portuguese, English, French, Geography, Science, Mathematics, History, Physical Education, Wood and Metal Technology. Several of my younger brothers and sisters followed this pattern of working and studying, for similar reasons.

The absolute highlight of this period in my life was in 1985 when I had turned 20. Sandra and I were among a group of young people selected to spend two weeks in Moscow representing our Timorese group. The focus of the visit was a youth festival where we performed and met many other young people from all over the world. I met some young men from Mozambique and was delighted to hear about the country of my grandfather. We stayed at the Sevastopol Hotel where we had our own phone, tried vodka, and visited many exciting places including Lenin's Tomb and the amazing Orthodox churches. The memories of our two weeks in Moscow are still with me.

My first full-time job was preparing the molten lead to cover the cables used in electrical works. The furnace operated 24 hours a day and the workers all rotated through morning, afternoon and night shifts. It was good money and I continued in this job for three more years. Two years later, at the age of 22, I became engaged to Sandra just before I was required to begin my compulsory military service.

I enjoyed army life so much that at the end of the two years, I signed on to join the permanent army and make this my career, becoming a member of the Portuguese Special Forces and, fortunately, being stationed near Balteiros camp where Sandra, Dad and the children were still living.

In 1990, my family moved into a permanent home. Milton, one of my younger brothers, remembers the excitement of the day they moved. 'When the day came to move into our own proper house we were all so excited. For 10 years we had been cramped into a small space and, although grateful that we had been provided with a safe and secure place, when we walked through the front door of our own house, I did feel relief. We all walked from one room to the next, going through every door, exploring every space. For 10 years we had lived in that army tent, and many months of fleeing from conflict before that time. I had almost forgotten what it felt like to live safely in a real house, our house!'

On the 12 November 1991 Sandra and I were married at a civil ceremony. Soon after, we learnt that on the same day, Indonesian army officers had fired on unarmed, pro-independence Timorese students in a protest at the Santa Cruz cemetery in Dili. At least 250 students were killed.[6] A video of what happened was smuggled out so the nations of the world could no longer ignore what was happening in our beleaguered country. In commemoration of the innocent students who had been gunned down, Sandra and I decided to postpone our church wedding and family celebration for a month, till the 12 December.

---

6 https://en.wikipedia.org/wiki/Santa_Cruz_massacre

Earlier, in 1980, my sister Maria and her husband Nuno Madeira were the first to migrate to Australia, seeking better opportunities for themselves and their future children. Mario followed in 1982 and together, Maria and Mario began sponsoring the rest of the family. Other members of the family followed over the next few years.

But it was a long time before we were all reunited in the same country because the Australian government did not accept migrants who had a disability. My sister, Ligia, was disabled and my brother, Pascoal, had poor sight in one eye caused by an accident when a child. Not to be deterred—nothing could deter my father after the life experiences he had been through—his determination and perseverance over ten years was eventually rewarded in 1996 when all his family was back together again, this time in Australia.

❖❖❖

Words cannot describe what our parents did for us. They always worked hard to provide us with a good life, and always ensured that we received an education. They maintained a calm authority even as we faced incredibly dangerous situations during our escape from the the civil war. My Dad lost his life mate, my Mum, under tragic circumstances. He later told us that Mum's last words to him were 'My journey is ending. I can't continue. Look after our kids.' And Dad did, continuing on to ensure that we were all together, that we were safe, educated, and secure.

Although the conditions were very basic and the future was uncertain, our time in the Balteiros refugee camp, living together with a large number of Timorese from all parts of our country as well as refugees from other former colonies, motivated us to explore our creativity and celebrate our heritage. We started a band and our music flowed; it has been heard all the way from 1980 to today. We now play a variety of wonderful tunes including modern music, traditional East Timor music, and the music of our grandfather's family background in Mozambique. I love hearing the music that we make, especially when we celebrate and share our traditional East Timorese music and include Timorese instruments.

I identify myself as being both Portuguese and Timorese. I did not apply to become an Australian citizen until now because in the back of my mind I had always thought and hoped that we would be able to return to an independent Timor one day. I acknowledge Mozambique as part of my past, the country and culture of my paternal grandfather. I am proud to be Timorese, and acknowledge that I was born a citizen of Portugal. But I have now decided that I am ready to take out Australian citizenship.

Santos Family

Berta Santos

My father, Joaquim Ferreira, whose mother was Timorese and father Portuguese, had studied in Italy in the 1930s and returned to East Timor as an agricultural engineer. His first job was teaching Portuguese to Chinese businessmen, afterwhich he moved to Loes, in Maubara, to work in a government agricultural program where one of his responsibilities was importing some agricultural machinery from Italy. This is where he met my mother, Maria do Carmo Nunes (Olo Doti), a local Timorese woman. They married, had their first child Joao; I was born later on 20 December 1942, the same year the Japanese invaded Timor.

The impact the Japanese occupation had on my family was devastating. My parents had lots of animals, including pigs and horses. My mother told me that Japanese soldiers would come to our house and take our pigs; and after some time, they rounded up all the people of Portuguese background to take them away to Liquica. My Timorese grandfather encouraged my father to hide nearby while my mother, my brother and me, still only a baby, lived with my grandparents. Unfortunately, while in hiding, my father developed malaria and became very ill. He sought help from the local priest who took him to the hospital in Liquica, where he later died. My brother Joao was only two at the time, and I was six months old.

Four years later, my mother remarried—to the *Liurai* of Gugleur—the village chief, Domingos Goncalves, in the district of Maubara, leaving my brother and me to continue living with my grandparents, about three hours away by horseback. As a result, we were only able to see our mother from time to time. Domingos had been the *Liurai* during the Japanese occupation, which had put him in an invidious position at times when the Japanese army demanded he supply men to work for them, or horses and pigs. Obviously, he felt he had no choice but to fulfil their demands.

Years later following the defeat of Japan, when the Portuguese resumed their rule of Timor, my stepfather and his cousin, Manuel Fino, were accused of cooperating with the enemy and imprisoned on Atauru Island, a very harsh place to be imprisoned. Not surprisingly, Domingos did not survive the experience, but his cousin was fortunate to get out of there alive and, as a qualified architect, went on to design several of the fine buildings in Dili. I was six years old when my stepfather died and at the time, my mother was pregnant with my half-sister. Fortunately for her, Domingos had arranged to provide a part of his coffee plantation for his unborn child, Maria Goncalves.

My mother and Maria came to live with us at my grandparents' home in Maubara. Although she had no money, she did have some well-bred horses which Joao and I loved looking after, including taking them to water. As a consequence, we became skilled horse riders. My mother made saddles for us which consisted of a cushion with several attachments: a girth going under the horse's belly, a strap going under the horse's tail, and the two stirrups. The saddles and bridles were all made from local materials, including the cushion which was stuffed with cotton from the local kapok tree; the bit to go in the horse's mouth was made from copper.

When we were of school age my mother's sister, Inocencia (Brumana), took my brother and me to live in a village near Ponilala in the Ermera District where we stayed with my mother's cousin, Adao Exposta, on her large coffee plantation called 'Ramera'. My aunt, my brother and I lived separately from the family, even having our own kitchen. Each day we walked one hour each way to attend school, and I remember walking along in the torrential rain that bucketed down during the monsoon season, using palm leaves as my only protection. We only returned home to our mum and family in Maubara for the three months of the summer school holidays.

When I was about 12 years old, the school at Ermera Vila burnt down, so my mother arranged for me to attend boarding school in Soibada—by this time, my brother was already boarding at a boys' college in Maliana. At one stage when my mother didn't have sufficient funds to pay the school fees, she approached the local Maubara *Liurai*, Gaspar Nunes, who was also her cousin, and asked to borrow a little money until she could pay it back. The *Liurai* said, 'Maria, I will give you the money in exchange for your horse'.

My mother was not at all happy with this arrangement as her horse, Mate-ana Orfao, was considered to be a very special indeed and was the last foal from a well-bred mare, so worth much more than the amount she needed to borrow. However, desperate for the funds, she was reluctant to say no to this arrangement, ending up exchanging her horse for the balance of the school fees she needed.

Later on family members were proud to learn that at the next annual horse show in Dili on *Dia de Camoes* (10 June, National Day in Portugal), Mate-ana Orfao won First Prize. Hopefully, it was some consolation for my mother who had given away her beloved horse, and a gift from her first husband, my father.

I completed school when I was 13 and stayed at home in Maubara, working in the garden, looking after the animals and learning how to cook, weave, make baskets and sew. Some special items I made, I was able to sell locally. My brother initially helped the nurse in the local clinic then joined the Portuguese army.

In the late 1950s, at the age of 16, I went with my mother, my aunt and uncle on a family outing to Alieu, two days' ride away. The adults were going to meet the family of my cousin's fiancée and negotiate the marriage. On the way back near Bazartete, where we had planned to stay with family overnight, we met a young man who introduced himself as Luis. This was my first meeting with my future husband and the love of my life. He offered us all accommodation at the home where he was boarding. My aunt declined, explaining that we already had accommodation arranged. It turned out that my aunt's cousin, with whom we were staying, was Luis's godfather. I also learnt that he had trained and studied in Dili to become a nurse and was now working at the government clinic in Bazartete.

Over the next three years, a courtship was conducted along very formal lines. Luis wrote to me and the letters were delivered by the priest who was responsible for conducting mass in both Maubara and Bazartete. My grandparents, aunts and uncles had to agree to the match if it was to progress to marriage; and I was certainly aware of the many discussions that went on. Luis, being a public servant, was a positive as he had a guaranteed income. However, maybe he was not from a good family? Having to move every three years or so from one clinic to another was certainly considered a negative, too.

Meanwhile, Luis had been trying to meet or at least see me some other way. He knew where we attended mass, so one Sunday he and some friends arrived in a borrowed car and drove around looking for me and, as Luis told me later, he tried to take my photograph. Luis arriving in the village uninvited, surprised and definitely did not endear him to my aunt, who spoke of the strange man, not from our area, who had behaved badly.

It seemed that my mother's older brother and his wife were opposed to Luis being considered my future husband; while fortunately, my mother and her younger brother were in favour. So when Luis wrote to my family asking for permission to visit, my mother and her younger brother wrote back agreeing to it. The formal courtship could now begin. However, Luis had been told many tales about girls whose family came from Maubara; apparently Maubara girls were very traditional so a suitor needed courage. Another tale he was told was that when you visit, you must arrive early in the morning. It was this tall tale that was to lead to great embarrassment for me on the first meeting of our courtship.

On the day Luis chose to visit, my sister and I were out in the fields picking peanuts. Very early in the morning Luis and three friends were seen by my auntie arriving on horseback. My mother sent news of their arrival out to us in the fields.

There I was all hot and now bothered in my working clothes, and certainly not happy to meet Luis in that state. My sister ran back to the house to collect clothes and a wash bowl. Following a wash at the spring and a change of clothes, I greeted him and his friends who were now talking with my mother over cups of coffee. Many times over the years, Luis and I laughed about the circumstances of the first day of our courtship.

Following our civil marriage service, we stayed in Bazartete and Luis continued on as the nurse at the local clinic. It was there that our first child, Aida, was born. During Portuguese rule, all adult males were required to serve in the army for a two-year period, except public servants, who only had to serve for 18 months. Luis decided to arrange his army service and get it over and done with before we had more children. So, we moved to Dili where Aida and I lived with Luis's sister while Luis stayed in the army barracks, returning to stay with my mother in Maubara for the birth of our second child, Joaquim.

At the end of his army service, Luis worked in the Dili Hospital for a few months before being posted to Barique in Manatutu. Far away from any family and friends, I was very unhappy and became sick. Luis was supposed to stay three years at the Barique clinic, but he was so worried about my health that he asked for a transfer back to Bazartete and was fortunately, granted this request. We were very happy back there with family and friends nearby. Luis was very well-respected by everyone, particularly because he spoke their local dialect. Every three years when he was supposed to move on to another clinic, the local families petitioned the authorities, demanding that he stay. As a result, Aderito, Nelson, Gil, Luis and Teresa were all born in Bazartete.

Since the majority of our older children were now of school age, we moved back to Dili in 1973 so they would have the best possible educational opportunities. Luis began working with the *Delegacia de Saude* (Health Department) taking responsibility for administering vaccinations. For the next 12 months we were very happy all together; we were comfortable and living conveniently in the middle of the city.

However, all that changed following the *Revoluacao dos Cravos* (Carnation Revolution) in Portugal in April 1974; life in Timor would never be the same again. The new Portuguese Government announced that they would withdraw from all their colonies. In Timor, political parties formed in preparation for a new political future, and radicalised students returned from studying in Portugal, convinced that Timor should become independent immediately.

Luis remained neutral during the growing tensions, refusing to join any of the political parties: we could see how divisive it was becoming with splits forming within families and communities as members joined one of the three parties. Even though Luis remained neutral, many of our family and friends were members of the UDT party and would sometimes borrow our car to use on UDT campaigns.

In August 1975, the conflict in the streets had intensified so much that we decided it was safer for my daughter Maria, our eighth child, to be born at home rather than for us to risk going out to the hospital. Once again, with a new baby girl, I wanted to be with my mother. So Luis took me and our eight children back to Maubara, staying overnight with us, then intending to return to Dili the next day. By this time, however, members of UDT and Fretilin were fighting along the way so although he tried a few more times, he ended up going to the hospital in Liquica instead where his skills were in great demand due to all the fighting.

One day, Luis was called to attend a very sick man in Bazartete. The following details come from information that has been passed to me, and from letters I received from Luis. On the way, Luis was ambushed and captured by Fretilin forces who took him to Nicolau Lobato's house. Nicolau was a Fretilin leader and also a close family friend, being the godfather of our daughter, Teresa. Luis stayed with the Lobato family for two weeks and then was taken by a member of the family to Dili where he looked after the sick and injured members of Fretilin. This was a time where there would have been no choices open to him. His capture would have been a bonus for the Fretilin cause—someone who could patch up wounded fighters.

However, while there, some Fretilin people accused Luis of helping UDT members to escape from custody, so they placed him in prison. I received a letter from him one month later imploring me to stay with my mother and look after the children.

I have since heard that while in detention, Luis and a friend were seen listening to a radio, so were accused of betrayal and sent to prison in Alieu. Even there, Luis continued to use his skills, tending to his fellow prisoners. I now know that my Luis helped many, many people. He thought of his syringe as his gun and his tablets as his bullets. The last letter I received from him was dated 16 December 1975, one week after Indonesian forces invaded Dili. I am convinced that a Fretilin commander ordered Luis to be killed. His last letter was smuggled out of the prison in Alieu, and I received it 12 months later.

When the Indonesian army invaded in December 1975, my children and I were already hiding deep in the mountains of Maubara. From my mother's house we could look out over the ocean and see the Indonesian warships; my children thought it was great to see all these amazing ships. However, the adults knew that it was not safe to stay in our house with its iron roof that could be seen so easily. So, we removed the sheets of iron and, taking them with us, we fled to our farm high up in the hills. There, we used the iron roofing to build shelters which we covered with coconut palm leaves to camouflage them from the eyes of the invaders. My children, my mother, my aunt and others spent the next 18 months surviving there. We didn't see any soldiers, but we could hear bombs exploding and guns firing.

After 18 months, however, we were all becoming very thin and I began to wonder how much longer we would survive there. I knew that Joaquim Henriques, an elderly teacher from Dili, was sheltering among rocks nearby. Joaquim had known me when I was a child, so I visited him to ask his advice. After some discussion, we agreed that we should all surrender.

Like many of the women of Timor, I was forced to make a difficult and dangerous choice. What else was there to do? I could not lose my children in a fight that we would not win! Unfortunately, Joaquim didn't join us; I will never know the reason why, but he died some time later. I alone had to take responsibility for this dangerous move.

It was on the 24 June 1976, that we all walked together down the hill tracks to my mother's house, the adults carrying the younger children. Only the pigs saw us arrive; it was so quiet, no one was there. The Maubara village was totally destroyed. Everything that could be removed had been taken by looting Indonesian forces. We were very frightened because we could still hear the guns continuing to fire.

With my young brother, Tito, carrying a stick with a white tea towel attached, we continued on our way down until we could see the Indonesian soldiers. As we approached them, we were surprised to see that many had shaved heads which made us think of men in prison, not soldiers. My mother whispered to me, fearfully, 'Look what you have done! You have brought us all to die. All your children are going to die.'

We had no common language so could not communicate effectively with them, but we were very relieved to learn that my uncle, the *Liurai* of Maubara, Gaspar Nunes, was there—it was Gasper who had taken my mother's special horse in exchange for the balance of the school fees when I was 12 years old.

We learnt from Gasper that as a UDT supporter he had fled the Fretilin forces and gone across the Indonesian border to Atambua. Later, when the Indonesians invaded Timor, they arranged for Gasper and other important people to be brought back to Dili. He had then asked to return to his home in Maubara.

The Indonesian soldiers told us to look for a place to set up our shelter. We noticed that people were trying to cook without any equipment or utensils, so my Aunt Inocencia, my brother Tito and my two cousins, returned to my mother's house to collect the necessary pots and utensils. On the way, however, they were captured by Fretilin forces and my cousin, Cornelio, was killed. The others chose to remain with the Fretilin forces for two years until Aunt Inocencia and her daughter were forced to surrender to the Indonesians. Tito avoided capture, fleeing into the bush where he stayed until he was forced to surrender several years on in 1979. Many years later, Tito became the Director of Land and Property in the District of Liquica and is still in that position today.

Rice was distributed by the Indonesian soldiers, and we cooked using improvised utensils, managing as best we could. I was still breastfeeding Maria. At this time, we met many Chinese women and their children whose husbands had supposedly been taken to work in Indonesia. It was only later when my aunt was praying at a church that she noticed Chinese clothes lightly covered with soil and discovered, what we now think, were the remains of the Chinese men.

It was obvious that our lives were in the hands of the occupying Indonesian forces, so in order for my family to survive, I set about making myself useful. We were asked if anyone could sew as the Indonesian soldiers needed their uniforms altered. All the sewing machines in Maubara had already been stolen so I said that I couldn't do that job. They also needed a nurse. I had often accompanied Luis when he worked in the clinic, and knew the basics so I volunteered for that position, insisting that my cousin also work with me even though he had no experience. I felt I needed him for my protection and soon taught him the basics. While we worked in the clinic, Mum looked after the children. My cousin and I quickly learnt how to understand basic, sometimes crude, signs indicating what medical complaint the patient had. We also learnt to remain serious and professional at all times as chatty behaviour could so easily be misinterpreted as inviting familiarity.

My children adapted to the new situation and when Indonesian teachers arrived, Aida, my eldest, started going to an improvised school where she began learning Bahasa. Joaquim, still a small boy, became a water carrier, having to get the water up from the one village well. An Indonesian soldier wanted to adopt Joaquim, but there was a firm 'no' from me to this request! Little Luis learnt to sing the Indonesian national anthem in his beautiful little voice which clearly enchanted the soldiers because they would give him something small—pieces of sardines or some rice. This is how we survived! Many children and old people died during the 18 months we were in this concentration camp. But we also observed that the Indonesian soldiers were often short of food themselves.

Many times, I asked for permission to take my kids to live in Dili but my request was not granted—I was needed as the only experienced nurse in Maubara. One time an Indonesian Red Cross nurse arranged for me to take two sick kids to hospital in Dili; I took my baby Maria, and Nelson accompanied me to assist with the sick children. We travelled on a small boat and I was told that I would have to return to Maubara in eight days' time. After taking the two sick children to the Dili hospital, Nelson, Maria and I went to our family house in Taibesi. Later, the Red Cross nurse called in to advise me that I should refuse to go back, and that I was so thin, that I would not survive if I returned to the camp in Maubara. He also brought us 10 coconuts.

After six days, the Indonesian police came to the house and told us that we had to go that night to stay at army headquarters, ready to return to Maubara. I decided not to go; instead my brother-in-law and my two nephews arranged for all three of us to stay in a very small house that was empty at that time. My brother had been able to rescue some items from our family home before it was looted by the Indonesian forces. As a consequence, he was now able to give me our fridge with a freezer compartment, my sewing machine and three chairs. And so, we started a business: we began with the making of icy poles, and once the sewing machine was fixed, I sewed clothes.

Four months later, my mother and the rest of the children were able to come to live with us in Dili. Once again, as a matter of survival, my children became entrepreneurs at a very young age. With a hand-sewn money bag hanging around their necks, they would go out into the streets selling icy poles. Some of the Chinese merchants from Bazartete who had been our friends and were grateful to Luis for his medical attention to their families, were also now living in Dili. They showed their gratitude by supporting me and my children by giving Nelson a job helping with the transport of supplies as my business developed, and providing me with six kilos of bones and two kilos of meat each week from their restaurant supplies, to sell on their behalf. With this, I was able to provide protein for my family and make a small amount of money.

My mother and all the members of the family living with us helped to prepare and sell what we made. We set up a stall in front of our house selling sugar, coffee, drinks and whatever we could make; and the priest allowed Nelson to set up a stall on the veranda of the parish house where he sold exercise books, pens, erasers and other items. He got into the habit of counting out all the coins after each sale. The priest jokingly commented to me, 'When my parishioners see Nelson counting coins on the veranda of the parish house they may think that the parish has lots of money!'

Another opportunity arose when my husband's friends at the Dili Hospital arranged for us to supply the cakes to the hospital. This was a great break as it meant we received an ongoing order for two hundred small cakes to be supplied twice each week.

In 1978 it was arranged for Joaquim and Aderito to attend a seminarian boarding school run by the Portuguese Jesuits. This allowed the boys to continue their education in the Portuguese language and culture. Fortunately, I only had to pay for their food, which I managed to do from the profits of the business; and they were able to come home each weekend.

The Catholic Church, through Father Leao and Father Cunha, had re-established the Externato Sao Jose school in early 1977, with the aim of maintaining a Portuguese-speaking school in Dili. Firstly, Aida and later the younger children, were then able to continue their education in the Portuguese language. So this is how we all survived from the second half of 1976 through to early 1979.

My Chinese friends told me of their plans to join their three daughters living in Australia who were prepared to sponsor them. They urged me to go with them to Jakarta and from there go on to Portugal. I was torn between staying with my children or escaping to safety. I sought counsel from Father Joao Felgueiras, a Portuguese priest. He encouraged me to leave so that I could tell the world what was happening in

Timor-Leste and create the opportunity to bring my children to safety. 'This war is not finished. There is more blood to be shed,' he predicted.

With that thought in my mind I found the courage to take the opportunity to leave my country, to leave seven of my children with their grandma, and escape taking only my youngest baby Maria, with me.

During those times the Indonesian authorities would allow Chinese and other foreigners to leave but definitely not the Timorese. My Chinese friends had to go to Jakarta, to the Australian Embassy, to arrange their visas to Australia, but they had two nieces whom they wanted me to take from Jakarta to their relatives in Portugal. My airfare to Jakarta was paid for by one Chinese merchant, and the list of his family's names was submitted including my name, in the hope that it would not be noticed.

Aida and my Mum knew that I was fleeing Timor, but my younger kids were told that I was going to Jakarta to buy some supplies. Father Joao brought Joaquim and Aderito from school to the airport to say goodbye which is when I told them that I was leaving Timor.

It was on 24 May 1979 that, with Maria in my arms, I left my seven children behind with their Grandmother to escape the violence surrounding us and hopefully, once in the free world, I would be able to arrange for my children to join me.

Arriving in Jakarta, we stayed with the family of our Chinese friends and they continued to support me. While they organised their migration to Australia, I visited the Dutch Embassy in order to seek asylum in Portugal. The processing of visas to Portugal had to be conducted at the

Dutch Embassy at that time as Portugal and Indonesia had no formal relations since Portugal did not recognise Indonesian rule of East Timor.

I had some funds, but my Chinese friends paid the balance of my airfare to Portugal and I was able to do a little in return by taking their two young nieces with me. I never did know whether any bribe money was paid by my Chinese friends to the Indonesian authorities to allow me to travel safely to Portugal. Either way, five months after arriving in Jakarta, in October 1979 with my baby, I finally escaped Indonesia and flew to Portugal without a hitch. During our five months in Jakarta, I had no news of my children left behind in Dili.

On arrival in Portugal, I lived in Pensao Flor, a hotel paid for by Catholic Mission, until I was able to find accommodation that I could afford. While I was there, Jill Jolliffe, the Australian freelance journalist[7], who had been a good friend of my husband came to the hotel to meet me. We struck up a friendship immediately and from then on, Jill became a great friend, and supported me throughout my mission to be reunited with my children.

From time to time, I found comfort in visiting Timorese families in Balteiro which was an area in Portugal that housed Timorese refugees as well as refugees from the many former Portuguese colonies, including Angola and Mozambique.

By a chance encounter, I met the son of a Portuguese army captain, Rui Fernando Texeira Lopez, who was looking for a Timorese woman to care for his 90-year-old mother, Mrs

7 Australian journalist and author, who famously reported and wrote a book on the Balibo Five which was made into a film: *Cover-Up:The Inside Story of the Balibo Five* (2001).

Amalia da Veiga. We discovered that there was a close family connection with Mrs Amalia. She had lived in Timor as a child and her father had been one of the people who had built the Church in Maubara—the Church I attended as a child, and which is still standing today. In March 2011, it celebrated its centenary, and I was there to commemorate this milestone.

I went to work for the Texeira Lopez family, living in and caring for their elderly mother. However, always on my mind were thoughts of my seven children and how I could get them to join me in Portugal. For the next three years I didn't cease to lobby for us to be reunited under the Family Reunification Act. Members of the Lopez family, their friends and their neighbours supported and guided me during this time; I was so fortunate to have made contact with these people because many of them were people of influence and some had worked in Timor.

Then a possible avenue opened up. Two American senators were visiting Portugal at the time, and Jill Jolliffe advised me to ask them for help, assuring me that these influential politicians had the power to organise permission for my children to escape Timor.

Jill followed up and contacted them and explained my circumstances. They promptly agreed to meet me. They asked for my children's photos and identification, and then said they needed a letter from the Portuguese government stating that they were willing to have my children living permanently in Portugal—only with that, they said, would they be able to arrange for my children to fly out of Dili.

So now where to go and who to see to get such a letter! Once again, a friend of the Lopez family was able to guide me. He had a contact in the Portuguese Border Control office where I arranged an appointment. At my first visit they agreed to write the letter for me. On my second visit I signed the letter, then collected it on my third visit. Thus armed, I visited the US Embassy where I was scanned by security officers and promptly told that they could only accept a letter in English. They referred me to where I could get a list of translators. Confused because of my lack of English, I went home.

Next day back to the US Embassy, again scanned, and this time I was able to understand what was needed. Jill Jolliffe recommended a translator, a Mrs Robin, who not only arranged the translation but lodged it with the US Embassy on my behalf. At last I had successfully navigated the bureaucracy of both Portugal and the US!

Finally, in July 1982, more than three years after I left Timor, the International Red Cross arranged for my children to leave Timor. First, they were flown to Denpasar where they stayed overnight before boarding a Qantas 747 which flew them to Jakarta. Aderito remembers, 'It was a huge plane full of Australians and Europeans. Joaquim and I had been in a seminary school for several years and were not prepared for the bad behaviour of some of the other passengers. We were shocked to see them kissing and cuddling, behaviours which today we think are acceptable, of course. From Jakarta we flew Swissair on to Zurich. It was in Zurich that a bag handler was surprised that seven children were only carrying two small bags. We told him that we were poor and that what was in those two cases were all the belongings we had. Our flight to Lisbon was a TAP Portuguese airline and we were the only Timorese on the plane.'

Gomes Family

L to R: Amandio, Bernardo, Carmelita and Elizabete Gomes, Mozambique 1974.

Storytellers Amandio Gomes and his daughter, Carmelita, Melbourne 2018.

Baptista Family

Storyteller Pedro Baptista, Melbourne 2018.

Maria and Antonia Baptista, Melbourne late 1990s.

Boavida Family

Back row L to R: Henrique, Meireles, Ligia, Octávio, Maria, Arthur, Mário. Front row L to R: Filomeno, Cândido, Jaime, Pascoal, Damião, Elivis, Milton, Portugal 1978.

L to R: Storytellers Milton and his brother Meireles Boavida, Melbourne 2018.

Santos Family

Back row L to R: Verissimo Morato (District Administrator), Berta, Luis, Nelson Alferes Matos (Army officer).
Front row L to R: Aida, Adérito, Joaquim, Timor-Leste 1970.

Storyteller Berta Santos, Melbourne 2018.

Bernardes Family

Back row L to R: Miguel Silva, Rui Bernardes, Aurete Martins, Francisco Bernardes, Milton Boavida, Sandra Boavida (née Bernardes).
Front row L to R: Ligia Silva, Joshua Silva (on knee), Jose Bernardes (grandfather), Ana Bernardes, Nathan Silva (on knee), Portugal 1999.

L to R: Storytellers Ligia Silva and Aurete Martins, Melbourne 2018.

Except for Alice, Emilia and baby, all in this photo were on the truck that travelle
from Dili via Ermera Vila to Atambua. (August 1975, see pp.127-157).
Back row L to R: Isabel, Jorio, Alice, Jorge, Maria, Jose, Tina.
Front row L to R: Emilia, Irene, Luzia and her grandson, Lenita, Melbourne 201

Storytellers Jose Florindo and sister, Emilia Roboredo with their mother, Isabe
Florindo. Melbourne 2018.

Napoleon Family

Grandma Rosentina Napoleon and six of the nine grandchildren who came with her to Australia. Back row L to R: Amelia Borges, Grandma Rosentina Napoleon, Ines Amarel, Maria Vieira, Maria Napoleon. Front row L to R: Paulo Vieira, Rosie Vieira. Photo was taken on wedding day of Ines, Melbourne 1983.

Storytellers Manuel Napoleon and sister, Maria Napoleon. Melbourne 2018.

Ceremony of the Order of Timor-Leste at the Treasury Building in Melbourne 2014. L to R: Amandio Gomes, Shirley Shackelton (wife of Greg Shackleton, one of the Balibo Five), Berta Santos, Francisco Carvalho.

Luis Napoleon, father of the storytellers Maria and Manuel Napoleon. Luis drowned at sea in the 1970s when working on ships. Photo taken Singapore Harbour 1969.

The plane landed, and so my children Aida, Joaquim, Aderito, Nelson, Gil, Luis, and Teresa were finally reunited with their little sister Maria and with their Mum. My overwhelming feeling of joy could not be imagined. I can't describe it. So many tears.

Gradually, we got to know each other again. Slowly, the memories of the years of separation dimmed.

Teresa Santos

A tribute to my mother.

My mother, Berta, is a remarkable woman who feels a deep solidarity with the people of Timor-Leste. She has a strong focus on social justice and peace, and works with pride to contribute to Timor-Leste's struggle for self-determination and nationhood.

The plight and suffering of the Timorese people was never far from her mind when Berta decided to migrate to Australia: she could be closer to her country than if she stayed in Portugal. She was also aware of the long-standing friendship between Australia and East Timor, forged during the Second World War when the Timorese helped the Australian soldiers in their fight against the Japanese. In addition, Berta believed that Australia would offer better long-term opportunities for her children than Portugal.

We arrived in Melbourne on 24 July 1985 with high hopes and dreams after being sponsored by Berta's cousin, Jamie Lobo. Our first experience was the Enterprise Migrant Hostel in Springvale, where we were treated with respect and very well looked after. The hostel was filled with people from many different, rich cultures, and languages and the services were fantastic.

The next step, as Berta remembers, took us to Dandenong: 'We rented a house in King Street, near the Dandenong Market, because I never wanted to experience again the days when we didn't have enough food'.

Then after only one year we received a Housing Commission home in Endeavour Hills where Mum continues to live today. We linked up with the Timorese Community in Melbourne whose members helped with our initial settlement experience. The Timorese Association gave us a voice and a sense of belonging, filling gaps in services and providing us with social and cultural opportunities. Maintaining a strong sense of community and taking pride in our heritage actually allowed us to gain a sense of understanding and appreciation of the other cultures that make up multicultural Australia.

Berta and her family love giving back to the community. I well remember when we arrived in Australia, we received a lot of help that made a wonderful difference in our lives. To be able to give back to the community that helped me grow up, who welcomed me, is very important to me.

Like many in the diaspora, my mother missed her motherland terribly: she missed the family left behind and she yearned for a free and independent Timor-Leste. One way was to be the voice of those in anguish. So Berta and we, her children, became political activists; her strength and commitment inspired us to devote our time to the cause, too, and together we became actively involved in all aspects of Timor and its journey to independence.

In 1986, Berta was the voice that was heard on 3CR Community Radio, broadcasting in Tetum for the Timorese community in Melbourne. Once a week for two years, Berta would travel 40 minutes to the city to broadcast news and updates of her beloved motherland.

But she wanted to share all facets of Timorese culture with a wider audience, so as a family we joined the Timorese Association of Victoria (TAV), which travelled throughout Victoria performing, dancing, and sharing songs of our culture. She wanted to educate, to introduce our customs and traditions to the wider Australian community, to build awareness of who we are and of our struggle.

Berta was also an active participant in Fretilin activities in Melbourne, playing a major role in organising fundraising functions to support the independence movement: coordinating events to welcome Jose Ramos Horta, Xanana Gusmão, Alkateri, Professor Noam Chomsky and many others. She attended pickets and demonstrations organised to voice the struggle going on in the small island to the north.

She was also very feisty: despite her political activities, my mother took the risky decision to visit Timor three times during the Indonesian occupation. On her first visit, she was presented at the arrivals hall with a card which said in Indonesian Bahasa language, 'You are welcome to Timor'. She was met by her brother-in-law and stayed in Dili for two days. Then armed with her 'Welcome' card, she went to visit her mother who was living back in Maubara. It was an incredibly emotional reunion. Berta told us later that, 'My mother was so poor, she lived so simply, but seemed content'.

The Indonesian Security and Control caught up with her the next day, when she was visited by an official who told her that she should have registered in each District she visited. Berta's defence was her 'Welcome' card. But that was not acceptable to the official who warned her: 'Next time follow the correct procedure, or you will be in trouble'. On her way back to Dili she did register at each District post and each time was asked to explain why she hadn't registered on the way in. Maybe she had become so used to the freedom to travel anywhere in her adopted country that she was finding it difficult to adjust!

On each subsequent visit, she found that family members and friends were reluctant to talk openly, fearing later repercussions.

In 1999 when at last the Timorese were granted the right to a vote on the future of their nation, my mother once again was active in assisting and guiding members. There were three places in Melbourne where the Timorese could register to vote, and then a month later they were able to return to lodge their vote. Berta worked at the Dandenong Centre, and at times I helped out. To register, people had to provide documents to show where they were born. This was often difficult and stressful for those who had fled for their lives without documentation, and others such as the Chinese East Timorese, who had never had such papers—many had to visit the local police station and sign a statutory declaration stating where they were born. When they saw Berta at the Centre, however, people felt reassured as she was so well known throughout our community.

In August 1999, after the referendum and during the Indonesian and militia backlash, Berta was involved with the

Australian army Language Training Program in Point Cook as part of the team that taught members of the Australian army who were going to work as peacekeepers there, how to speak and write in Tetum.

The rampage following the referendum was a horror that unfolded before the eyes of the world. Mobile phones meant that the brutal killings and destruction being perpetrated across the country on a mass scale could be communicated in real time to the world.

Hundreds of Timorese were forced to flee their homes, taking shelter from the Indonesian army and militia wherever they could. And hundreds fled their country by whatever means of transport out they could find and were offered refuge in Australia. In Victoria, the Puckapunyal army base served as emergency accommodation for many of those fleeing.

My mother and other Timorese spent a few months living there supporting them. Initially, she was interpreting and assisting the new arrivals as they were vaccinated and given health checks, and trying to adjust to the strange surroundings and the different daily routines. Schools were quickly set up for the children, and Berta began working as a teacher aide in the classrooms. Later she commented that, 'The medical and dental staff at the Puckapunyal army base did a wonderful job. Many refugees had longstanding eye problems corrected, teeth were inspected and treatment given, and some children with cleft palates had corrective operations.'

◈◈◈

My mother's house, like her heart, is open to all: to help, and to welcome those in need. In 1996, she had taken in a young Timorese man named Jose de Costa. He had escaped from Indonesian-occupied Timor-Leste in a makeshift boat. Several years later, following independence, Jose returned to Timor-Leste where he has since taken parts in films and documentaries, and is now a director in the fledging film industry of Timor-Leste.

My mother reflects happily that, 'I now live in Endeavour Hills, my eight children are all grown up and have produced many wonderful grandchildren. My children are educated, and we live in a safe country. For more than three of their early years, my children grew up without their mother; however, I had no choice but to make that sacrifice, and it has all paid off. We are all together now; we were separated and then came back together again. Life is good. I enjoy living here, in Australia.'

In 2017, Berta received the *Ordem de Timor-Leste* (Order of Timor-Leste) in recognition of her contribution to the people of our country. Taur Matan Ruak, President of Timor-Leste, was in Melbourne to present the medal. I attended the special ceremony and had the honour of receiving the medal on behalf of my amazing mother.

Berta still travels around Australia, mostly on invitation, to share her inspirational story of determination, hope and faith.

Bernardes Family

FERNANDO BERNARDES

Aurete Martins tells her father's story.

Born within the grounds of the S. Jorge (Saint George) castle in Lisbon my father, Fernando, grew up during the rule of Antonio de Oliveira Salazar (1932-1968), the Portuguese dictator who exercised vast political powers. From an early age, Fernando developed a lameness in one leg. The family explanation of this disability was that when one year old, he had been left sitting on a piece of cold marble for a long time. Apparently, the sciatic nerve 'froze' and his leg didn't develop. Whether this was the cause or not, my father always had to walk with a stick, even as a boy, and was landed with the nickname, *Fernando Côxo* (Fernando, the Lame).

His family was very poor, so his childhood was very tough: he had to go out each day looking for food or for work—there were no concessions around his disability. His father's code was, 'If you return home empty handed, then you don't eat!'

As a young man in his early twenties, Fernando came to the radical view that one person, Antonio de Oliveira Salazar, should not have such total power at the expense of the ordinary people. This realisation led him to became involved in anti-Salazar movements until eventually, he was part of an unsuccessful assassination attempt on the life of the dictator. Along with other co-conspirators, Fernando was caught and given what would have seemed like a death sentence at the time: exile as a convict to Portuguese Timor, the penal colony as far removed from Portugal as was possible.

On the ship that transported him to that far-flung destination, Fernando met another political prisoner, Manuel Carrascalão. Thus, began a friendship which developed into a life-long close bond.

On arrival they were both placed in the same jail in Aipelo (the ruins of this building I have seen on a visit back to Timor). Later, they were released on good behaviour bonds but were exiled from their homeland for life and were not allowed to leave the colony. So, they started new lives, embracing the opportunities available, marrying Timorese women, settling down and having children. Fernando married Carolina Martins who came from Tilumar in Cova Lima District.

My father was a man of many skills; he had been a tailor, a photographer and a mechanic, and over time, developed a taxi business. The youngest of seven girls, I was born in Dili in 1940 and was only two years old when the Australian and the Japanese soldiers arrived in our country. When the Japanese began occupying Timor a few families got together and moved away from Dili to Liquica. It was at this time that Fernando and his friend in exile Manuel Carrascalão, made their pact: 'If anything was to happen to either of us, the widow and children would become the responsibility of the remaining one'.

My father would become outraged when the Japanese soldiers raided the markets, snatching all of the best fresh fruits without paying. The stallholders were all local farmers who had put their hard work and effort into growing the produce but were too scared to remonstrate with the soldiers knowing that they would be killed if they did. My father wanted so badly to get back at those thieves that he thought up a plan to punish them.

He picked some bananas from his own trees and injected them with a poison that a pharmacist friend had given him. Then he took them to the market and placed them on a stall which he knew the Japanese soldiers always stole from as was their practice. Sure enough, when the soldiers arrived they raided the market, including stealing some of Fernando's bananas. Then as usual, they sat under a tree to eat their stolen booty.

The poison would have taken at least two or three hours to take effect, so well after the soldiers had moved away from the market. And probably, the sickness that developed would have been attributed to malaria or some other local fever rather than associated with the market produce.

By this time Manuel Carrascalão had developed a coffee plantation which he called 'Fazenda Algarve', named after the place where he had grown up. My parents thought the occupying Japanese soldiers' behaviour was immoral and cruel because they terrorised and innocent the families. To escape this, my family and others fled to the Carrascalão plantation where an underground shelter had been constructed. If Japanese soldiers were sighted or their military planes flew over, then everyone took shelter underground.

At the same time, Australian soldiers were scattered across Timor, hiding in the jungle, only ever seen in small groups. Sometimes they rested with our families at the plantation and I remember them arriving, carrying everything they had, often bringing us sugar and tins of condensed milk. In return, my mother and the other women cooked them meals. One soldier would always be on duty looking out for the enemy. When the group left, they would just vanish into the vegetation.

Japanese soldiers would also come to the plantation from time to time and stay for a few days, looking for Australians, but we always denied seeing them. To associate with the 'enemy' was extremely dangerous as the Japanese were known to kill all the people in a village if they believed Australians had been helped.

While I remember that we were always in fear of the Japanese soldiers, there were two officers who were different—they were friendly and kind. One gave my friend, Alice Carrascalão, a pet bird, a beautiful lorikeet; I wanted to have one, too, so next day he brought me one, but at the same time Alice's bird had disappeared. I have always wondered whether it was the same bird, recycled!

Eventually, the Japanese took all the families prisoner, making us walk for miles without adequate food and shelter, from one village to another. During this trek, my father never stopped still with us, instead, mounted on his horse Germano, he would ride off looking for food and materials for shelter, which he would bring back to us. At the same time, Manuel Carrascalão was always with us as we were moved from one place to another. My parents had seven daughters at this stage but two of my sisters died from diphtheria as, of course, there was no medicine available to them.

Fernando had been warned that Japanese soldiers were looking for him, but he continued to move from one place to another looking for food for us all, managing to hide from the Japanese for some considerable time.

Eventually though, we received the devastating news that my father had been killed. The Carrascalão plantation was one of the few places that had a phone and Mary, daughter of Manuel, overheard a crossed line conversation saying that Fernando the Lame had been killed by the Japanese. Apparently, he had been betrayed by his mechanic who told the Japanese that my father was responsible for poisoning some soldiers. It seems that the motivation for this betrayal by his emplyee was the takeover of Fernando's business which the mechanic then took as his own.

We heard later that the Japanese soldiers came for my father, who at that time was well out of Dili in Remexio, on the road to Manatutu. They seized him, tied him to the tail of his horse. The horse panicked and galloped off back towards Dili. Fernando's body would have been bounced and bashed all along the way, causing him unimaginable pain and suffering. Once Germano made it to Dili and the soldiers had caught him again, they untied my father who was still alive, barely; and Germano ran loose, galloping all the way back to Fazenda Algarve, the Carrascalão plantation in Liquica. The horse's arrival at the plantation confirmed for everyone that Fernando had been killed.

Back in Dili, the soldiers dragged Fernando onto Farol beach, where other bodies had been left, and placed him face up on the sand, positioning his arms and body in the shape of a cross. Then they tortured him by using a bayonet to stab him all over his body. At the sound of a bell starting to ring, they stabbed him through the heart, ending his life.

What were his last thoughts as he lay waiting to die? As thoughts of his wife and daughters flooded through his mind, at least he would have taken some comfort knowing that his friend, Manuel Carrascalão, would take good care of them.

In those days the area around Farol beach was covered in trees, bushes and grass. As it happened, there were two men hiding up a tree who witnessed the torture and death of my father: Juarez, a Portuguese friend of my father, and Stevenson, an Australian commando. Years later, the friend told my mother that it was a Sunday market day and the bell was rung to indicate the opening of the market. It appears that my father was killed at 11 a.m.—in time for the soldiers to go to the market.

Juarez waited until dark, then took my father's body to the Santa Cruz cemetery where he buried him. Unfortunately, all we know about the position of his grave is that it was near a wall.

In 1973, Stevenson returned to Timor, bringing his son with him. They had lunch at my sister's house because he had known my sister's husband when he was in Darwin training as a paratrooper.

It was 15 August 1945. Someone had access to a radio and heard that a bomb had been dropped and the war with Japan was over. We were so very sad that my father had not lived to see the end of the Japanese occupation. At the same time, we were relieved that life once again could be free from fear. Manuel Carrascalão kept his pledge and took responsibility for the welfare of my mother and her children. We returned to live in our Liquica house but there was no school for my older sisters to attend. Never prepared to let things be when it came to the education of her children, my mother went to meet the Bishop, Jaime Garcia Goulart, to discuss the matter. He agreed that my four older sisters should attend the college in Soibada which had been set up to provide an education for orphans and children of poor families; but this meant they would have to leave home and board at the school.

This was very hard for us all since we were too poor for them to travel home on holidays. It meant we were not to see my sisters until they were grown women. This must have been a very difficult decision for my mother to make: she was sacrificing family time with her daughters knowing that this was their only chance of a good education and training. From time to time, the Bishop passed on news of their welfare to Mum.

When I was seven, Manuel Carrascalão's daughter Alice, and I went to the Catholic boarding school in Ermera Vila; and when the older Carrascalão children were ready to attend secondary school, Alice and I moved with them to Dili where I completed my schooling, along with them. My mother had remarried so stayed on in Liquica, later on having three more children. Even though Mum now had the added responsibility of three more young children, she was always concerned about her older daughters' welfare, moving with her new husband and family to Dili some time later so she could see all her children.

At the age of 20, I moved to my sister, Ilda's, house and began work in the government finance department in Dili, on weekends often attending soccer matches with my sister and brother-in-law. That was where I first noticed Francisco, a handsome young Portuguese soldier who played a good game of soccer, too. He was based at the army barracks in Taibesse serving the required three-year military service from 1959 to 1962.

On Valentine's Day, in 1961, we both attended a 'Carnaval' Ball organised by a one of the sporting clubs, and were introduced to each other; after that, we danced together the whole night. Francisco and I were married on 21 October 1961, when I was 21 years old, and we immediately made arrangement to travel to Portugal where Francisco was to hand back his commission and formally leave the Portuguese army—and I was to meet his family.

Flying to Portugal was my first experience of being away from my homeland, so I was very lucky that Francisco's family made me feel very welcome, going to lots of trouble to prepare my favourite foods. Within a few weeks of arriving there, we had rented our own house in Torres Vedras, a city 42 kilometres from Lisbon and near Francisco's family. My husband got a job straight away, returning to the same position he had prior to military service. Everyone was delighted when Ligia was born in 1963. It was a happy time living in Portugal, feeling an important part of Francisco's family.

We could have stayed and made a life there, but Francisco and I decided that job opportunities were better in Timor. So in September 1964, with Ligia now 18 month old and me pregnant with our son Rui, we returned to Timor and slipped easily back into life in Dili. Francisco, now a civilian, didn't have any difficulty finding a job.

Mr Brito, the BNU (Portuguese Bank) Bank Manager, had several enterprises going in Timor. He wanted to set up a tyre factory and my uncle, knowing of Francisco's previous experience working in a tyre business while in Portugal, recommended him to Mr Brito. Francisco was offered the manager's position, but unfortunately the tyre business didn't eventuate. Feeling obliged to offer Francisco another position, Mr Brito engaged him in another of the bank's enterprises where he was responsible for maintaining the supply of construction materials.

My life back in Dili centred on two young children and the home, back in the bosom of the family: my Mum, my sisters and their children all lived nearby.

In 1965 my brother-in-law, Carlos Afonso Henriques, needed someone to work in administration in the *Obras Publicas*, (Public Service) so I applied for the job and was successful. Unfortunately, only six months after our return from Portugal when Ligia was only two years old, she developed an extreme allergic reaction to mosquito bites. The doctor advised us that she should go to a colder climate; that she would not survive if she stayed in Timor.

So it was arranged that my sister, Ilda, would take her by ship back to Francisco's Mum and Dad in Portugal to live. Imagine the heartbreak for everyone when the time came for our little daughter to leave. But there seemed no other option and we knew that she would be loved and cared for her by her grandparents, and that she would be safe and happy.

Francisco stayed in his job for two and half years before moving into a government job on the wharf. He was now responsible for organising the workers, the trucks and the tractors on the wharf. Ships would come into the port bringing in stores, mainly for Chinese businesses, which would be stored in the warehouses, waiting for collection.

I continued working at *Obras Publicas* for two more years, only taking one month of entitlement leave when Ana was born. Francisco and I employed a maid who looked after baby Ana and toddler Rui, and cleaned the house. When a vacancy in a government position at the wharf became available, I took it and later took advantage of job rotation opportunities, spending time in the Land and Property Department, before being promoted to being in charge of administration in the Motor Registration Department where I continued until 1975. During this time, our daughter, Sandra, was born in 1971.

As we were both working in government jobs, Francisco and I decided to allow our annual leave to accumulate for a few years so we could take Rui, Ana, and baby Sandra to meet their older sister, Ligia and their grandparents, in Portugal. We carefully saved our money and in 1973 we had a wonderful reunion with Ligia, who did remember Francisco and me, and was happy to meet her younger siblings. The nine months we were able to spend in Portugal was a very happy time getting to know our eldest daughter once again and spending time with Francisco's family.

Ligia Silva

Ligia will now tell her life story and also continue the family story from 1974, when we had all returned to East Timor.

My life began in Portugal in 1963. Living among my Dad's family, my first language was Portuguese. We moved to live in East Timor the next year; and it was expected that that was where I would be raised and would attend school. From an early age I was a tomboy, climbing everything I could—my nickname was appropriately, Macaca, meaning monkey.

When I was on the ship that took me to Portugal after I was diagnosed with an acute allergy to mosquito bites, I remember one experience that caused me trauma that was to stay with me during my early years. I was hanging over the edge from the hole where the anchor chain was set, looking into the ocean, watching the fish. My Aunt Ilda, concerned that I might fall in, told me that, 'Big fish will come and get you'. At that very same moment the ship's horn sounded and utterly terrified me—I thought it was the big fish coming to get me! I was terrified then and remained so each time I heard such a loud noise. For years after, if a car sounded its horn I would hide under my grandmother's skirts.

Looking back on those early years living with my grandparents in Portugal, I'm sure I was very spoilt, most of the time being the only child among several adults. My grandfather allowed me to do everything I wanted—in his eyes I could do no wrong. I'm pretty sure that at times I was very naughty!

One early memory that demonstrated a difference between life in Timor and life in Portugal was when I asked my grandmother for sweetcorn the way my mother had prepared it in Timor. Her reply was, 'Corn is not for children; it is only for animals'.

The summer months were very special and spent with my cousin, Carlos, who was one year older than me. His mother, my Auntie Helena, would rent a house at Santa Cruz, a seaside town about 12 kilometres away, and we loved spending the three months of the summer holidays playing together on the beach.

As I had left Timor when I was still a toddler, not surprisingly, my parents quickly became a faint memory as I enjoyed a privileged life in Portugal. When I next saw them, when they came to visit, I was already nine. My grandparents had not told me that they were coming—maybe they wanted it to be a grand surprise—so on the day they arrived, I remember walking home from school with my friend, and as we walked up the hill, my Dad was walking down towards us. I immediately recognised him, but I didn't know what to do, so I allowed him to pass without acknowledging him. I stared at my Mum, not allowing myself to be sure; but I did notice her lovely hair. Beside me, my friend commented, 'She's so pretty!'

And so, I was reunited with my parents and introduced to my little brother, Rui, and my two little sisters, Ana and baby Sandra. My parents had nine months' leave from their jobs so there was plenty of time to get to know my family. We rented a house in Torres Vedras and I remember we had a very happy time all together.

We all returned to Timor in February 1974, when I was ten years old. My first impressions of Dili as we came down the gangway from the plane was of smells: smells that triggered very early childhood memories. The smell of fires burning because everyone cooked over wood fires; the smell of delicious barbecued corn cooking; and the smell of the tropical fruit, lime.

This was a new stage in my life as I was to be reunited with my wider family and settle into life in Timor. We moved into Auntie Ilda's large house in Farol, by the beach, and I really enjoyed meeting up with my cousins again even though I had not remembered them. But I was also very homesick for life in Portugal. I missed my friends, my dog Cilai, my canary, my grandma and grandpa, the other aunties and, especially, cousin Carlos. Life moved on, however, and my schooling resumed as I began attending Grade 5 in *Ciclo Preparatorio* (middle school), continuing on to Grade 6 in 1975.

Dili was a small city, so everyone knew each other and shared their stories and information. I have since learnt that when the news came through of the coup in Portugal in April 1974, there was much discussion as to what that meant for Timor. We knew that people in Portugal were tired of losing their sons to civil conflicts and resistance movements in places like Angola and Mozambique, colonies so far from their homes. We knew of Timorese students returning from study in Portugal who came back with their socialist ideas. We knew of three Portuguese army officers who encouraged the Timorese students to demand immediate independence from the colonial power.

Political parties began to form in the community and develop their philosophies. The UDT party decided on a staged path towards independence over a ten-year period, while Fretilin wanted it to happen immediately. Tensions began to develop as people began to take sides. My strong memory of those times is being discouraged from talking about politics, especially outside the house; I did know, however, that my parents were supporters of UDT.

During the 1974/75 school year, my Grade 6 teacher was Nicolau Lobato, one of the Fretilin leaders. My family was concerned that the children from UDT families would be treated differently by him, but fortunately this did not happen. He was a great teacher who treated all his students fairly; we all loved him. Nicolau was later to become the first prime minister of East Timor during the very brief period in 1975 from 28 November to 7 December before the Indonesian army invaded. He then fled with other Fretilin leaders into the mountains and was, sadly, killed by Indonesian forces three years later.

Another memory was of being on a balcony watching angry and passionate people demonstrating with signs that said MATE BANDEIRA HUM which translated means 'Die on the shadow of the flag' (Fretilin flag). I was 12 years old and on school holidays: all this action was very exciting!

In July 1975 my parents decided that our house in Bairro

Pite which was near the former Dili airport, was too close to the conflict zone. I well remember times when my mother, driving our car with a UDT flag flying, had stones thrown at the car and windows punched by Fretilin supporters. We moved to a house near the BNU Bank and close to the wharf where my father worked. Of course as young children, we thought of this as an adventure; we were too young to fully appreciate the danger we were in.

One significant day in late August 1975, Dad had gone to work, to be greeted by his boss saying, 'What are you doing here? Don't you realise the danger you and your family are in! You have to pack them up now and take them to the wharf, and be ready to escape Dili on a ship!'

Dad jumped into a borrowed 4-wheel-drive and drove home as fast as he could. Coming to an abrupt halt, he raced into the house and, in a voice that invited no questions, told us, 'We have to leave the house now! Pack up only what is of value.'

I began packing my dolls and was upset when by Dad said firmly, 'No, you cannot take dolls'. In spite of that, I still managed to secretly take them. I remember Dad placing clothes on a bedspread, then bundling everything up and tying the corners together. That was the extent of our luggage. Alberto, our loyal Timorese servant, came with us too.

We drove the five minutes to the wharf and were one of the first families to arrive. We hadn't taken any food as we didn't think we would be staying long; we thought that once the conflict was over, life would return to normal and we would return home. Other families began to arrive over the next few days, till eventually, the warehouse was overflowing with families, all with very few possessions. Somehow, we managed to set ourselves up to sleep, eat and share this confined space in the overcrowded warehouse. Food was very limited, but everyone shared whatever they had. Tins of baby food and Coca-Cola were discovered in the warehouse which we all consumed. Alberto went back to our house to collect food but found the house already occupied by Fretilin members; he told us that he saw a truck taking some of our furniture away.

My parents became aware that the Portuguese navy commander had signalled a Norwegian ship that was passing by and requested that it rescue the people at the wharf and take them to Darwin. However, the captain of the ship was concerned about the fighting going on in Dili and refused to dock at the wharf.

Meanwhile, the Fretilin leaders had ordered the Portuguese officers to detain the men only, and let the women, children and old people go onto the ship. All the men including my father, were then detained in a warehouse; and we were told that cattle barges would come alongside the wharf and take us, one group at a time, out to the ship in the harbour: all women and children had to be loaded before midnight.

I remember it being chaotic, with barges going back and forth to the ship. My Mum left me on the wharf minding the three younger children while she tried to find Dad. What a difficult decision for my mother to make: take her children to safety and leave their father behind, or wait, hoping that the family could stay together. She decided that we would not leave without Francisco, our Dad.

It was well after midnight and the last barge had left so it seemed that we had missed our chance to escape. Fortunately, a wealthy Chinese merchant also wanted to leave, so another barge arrived. About this time Mum received a message that Dad was already on the ship, so she signalled that we were to board that barge. The perimeter of the area near where you boarded the barge was being looked after by a Portuguese army officer who supervised the boarding.

Our servant, Alberto, being male and Timorese knew he would not have been allowed to board. He was in tears, convinced that if we left him behind he would be targeted by Fretilin for having worked for a UDT family. It was dark when my mother approached the Portuguese army officer to distract him while Rui and I encouraged Alberto to leap off the wharf into the barge. The barge was to leave soon, which had myself and every other family there in a panic to get all their belongings into it, throwing their bags in from the wharf.

Soon after thinking that we were going to be left behind, I panicked and threw two-year-old Sandra down to Alberto who had made it onto the barge. At the same time, someone threw a bag which hit Sandra. I was horrified, convinced I had just killed my baby sister. At that moment, too, I realised that I had lost a bag of tinned food Mum had given me to mind. Fortunately, Sandra was okay and Mum was so relieved that we were all safely off the wharf and heading towards the ship, that the loss of a few tins of food paled into insignificance. Our family of seven were among the 1150 refugees rescued by the Norwegian ship that night. We left our home behind to the sound of gunshots in our beloved Dili.

How delighted, then, we children were when we discovered that our Dad was indeed on board with us. Dad's boss at the wharf knew the men would probably not survive a Fretilin attack, so had arranged for all the lights to be turned off, and under darkness, the men were released from the warehouse. They were then able to board barges which took them to the ship much earlier in the night than the women and children.

The ship was not built to accommodate the number of people who were crowded on board, but we managed as best we could. In our two families there were seven children all together—four in our family and three cousins in the other. Fortunately, beautiful baby Sandra attracted the attention of the ship's cook who gave us some soup. Each of us seven kids was given a spoonful in turn, and that was the only food we had on our night and next day voyage to Darwin.

Surprisingly, although we were in the tropics, out on deck where we slept that night got quite cold, and we had no warm clothes with us. Dad assembled a shelter using wooden pallets for walls and his jacket placed over the top for the roof. It was fun in our little tent cuddling together. We fell into a deep sleep, exhausted.

As soon as we arrived in Darwin, each family group was vaccinated and immediately taken by bus to accommodation in many different locations, so we lost contact with Mum's sisters and our cousins who had been on the same ship.

Darwin had been almost completely destroyed by Cyclone Tracey just nine months earlier, on Christmas Day in 1974. So the accommodation we were allocated for the first week was actually a destroyed primary school building. Each of us was given a bed, a towel, a comb, toothbrush and toothpaste and lots of food, including chicken and chips—with lots of chicken.

It was another exciting time for us kids with all our basic needs met, no chores and many children to play with. So cool!

The Australian authorities gave my parents the choice of going on to Portugal or choosing one of the Australian capital cities to settle in. My mother chose Perth—her decision was influenced by a friend living in Darwin who recommended we go there. We later heard that my two aunts, Fernanda and Albertina and their families, who had also escaped on the Norwegian ship, had decided to go on to Portugal.

We flew to Perth and settled into the Graylands Migrant Hostel where I began attending school with not a word of English. I remember feeling awkward and a little scared even though there were other Timorese refugees and some from Chile. The teachers were kind and helpful and the other students treated us well, too. I remember going on a school camp where we were canoeing on a river and being filmed by a journalist. As the journalist took photos of the 'refugee children', we had to continue waving.

We only stayed in Perth for three months; my Dad was not comfortable with the English language and he knew that his old boss in Portugal would have a job for him. Dad's forethought meant that we had the necessary passports, other documentation, and some money with us that he had thrown in with our belongings before we fled our house.

How to get to Portugal was the immediate challenge. Portuguese soldiers had also escaped Dili and were stranded in Darwin, so the Portuguese government sent a plane out to collect them. We flew back to Darwin to get on it, along with some other Timorese families, and arrived in Portugal on 25 November 1975.

I immediately felt as if I had come back home; to the place where I had spent so many happy childhood years. Now I realise that at that time, I identified more with Portugal than with Timor—understandably as I had spent most of my childhood from 18 months old to 10 years there.

It was wonderful seeing my Portuguese family and friends again; and once again, we rented a house in Torres Vedras. We all resumed school seamlessly as it was the same curriculum that was taught in Timor. Refugees were streaming in from Timor and from the other Portuguese colonies, all as a consequence of the descent into chaos in these countries that followed the new government of Portugal's decision to decolonise.

Initially, my Dad worked in a government job, but later, he retired early on a half pension and went back to work in the tyre business for his old boss.

After finishing high school, I worked in a range of jobs including selling books from door to door. However, because of the thousands of refugees that had flooded into Portugal since decolonisation, there was a shortage of employment opportunities. We had to look elsewhere for a better future.

Ten years after arriving back in Portugal in 1985 when I was 22 and my brother Rui was 21, we arranged to migrate to Australia, sponsored by my Auntie Albertina, who had left Portugal earlier along with many other family members. On arrival in Melbourne, I shared accommodation with my cousin Dulce, Auntie Albertina's daughter, and later with my cousins Fabiola and Diogo. We had never had formal English language classes, but over the years we had learnt some English from TV programs, pop songs and movies.

It was good to arrive in Melbourne and be reunited with many of our Timorese family members once again, but I had left behind my fiancé, Miguel, in Portugal, who was facing two years of compulsory military service. We set about arranging for Miguel and me to be married by proxy so that it would be easier for him to be accepted as a migrant to Australia.

With Mum and Dad still in Portugal, they were able to represent me with the Portuguese authorities. But to satisfy the Australian authorities, I had to find a guaranteed job for him, which I did. He arrived in Melbourne in 1986 and four years later, Mum, Dad, Ana and Sandra joined us. Sandra, the youngest, had the advantage that she had learnt English at school and was 19 when they migrated to Australia.

⟐⟐⟐

When I reflect on my life, I understand why, even today, I identify as Portuguese rather than Timorese. In those early years, I absorbed the Portuguese culture and was schooled in the Portuguese language. When I was taken back to Timor in February 1974, I attended school where Portuguese was the only language used, and I mixed with Portuguese children whose parents were working in Timor. Many of my teachers were Portuguese and some were wives of Portuguese army officers. I always spoke to my aunties, cousins, uncles and friends in Portuguese, and then in late 1975 when my family went back to Portugal.

I am not able to speak Tetum, the first language of the East Timorese though I do remember my mother speaking Tetum with our servant Alberto and with her sisters.

Florindo Family

Jose Florindo

Childhood for me was innocent and simple; tedious at times as there were several rules, but it was straightforward. There were eleven children in our family—Alice, Rosa, Jose, Luzia, Emilia, Irene, Tina, Maria, Jorio, Lenita and Jorge. I was the third child and the oldest boy, so I was required to take on considerable responsibility for the care of my younger brothers and sisters, as was our culture.

My Mum, Isabel, was born in Fatubessi, into a family whose father came from Maliana and whose mother was from Suai. She was the fifth child in the family and there were two other younger children. Daily life revolved around family and the provision of food, with each child having their daily chores.

My Dad, Zeca, had a Portuguese father and a Chinese mother from Macau, another Portuguese colony. Dad had attended school, so was literate in Portuguese; when my parents were married, Dad taught Mum how to read and write. Our home was in the village of Fatubessi, high up in the towering mountains of Timor, that allowed us to see over and beyond our limits.

Living with ten siblings was tiring at times but my family was remarkable. Our house was crammed, with four or five people at a minimum sleeping in one room. Despite this, the atmosphere was always bright and loving; food was always on the table, and laughter accompanied our daily lives. Living this contented life, we were unaware of the danger awaiting us around the corner.

Timor was a Portuguese colony so as a family, we enjoyed some of the privileges of having a Portuguese background. We all attended school and became literate in the Portuguese language. At first, we attended a primary school in our village but later, my family set up another family house in Ermera Vila so that all the children—my siblings and my cousins—could attend the Catholic primary school that offered a higher standard of teaching. From then on, we could only return home to Fatubessi on school holidays.

Most people in our village worked in the large coffee corporation SAPT, *Sociadede Agricola Patria Trabalho* (Agriculture Corporation for Work and Country) which had been established some time earlier by a retired governor of Dili. My father was able to work in the administration area because he was literate, while the local Timorese men and women worked on the coffee plantations that surrounded the village. Like my parents, many young men and women met their marriage partners while working for this corporation.

My memories are of a harmonious group of people. The children and youth respected their parents, their grandparents, and other adults, and accepted their authority. In my childhood, I never witnessed any crime. However, when I was a bit older, I do remember wondering about the absolute authority of the *Liurai*[8]: why the traditional leader

8 *Liu* meaning in charge; and *rai* meaning land.

of an area had such power, and noting that the local people obeyed the Liurai without question.

I also became aware of the fact that the majority of Timorese people lived with very little: their houses were made of bamboo and palm leaves and were just one room; and the floor was their bed and their table. When they worked for others, including the *Liurai*, they were paid very little or only paid with food. These observations developed in me a belief that this was not a fair system, that it should be changed.

In 1968, when I was aged ten, my parents decided that I should have the opportunity to attend a highly regarded Catholic boarding school in Soibada near Manatutu. There I met members of families who were to become influential in the destiny of East Timor: the Lopez De Cruz family, one of the founding families of the UDT Party; the Lobato family, who were leaders in Fretilin; and the Osorio Soares family, leaders in Apodeti.

Attending the boarding school was very hard for me. I had never been away from home before and missed my family hugely, and hated the food. Towards the end of the first school year in April 1969, I was so miserable and failing my studies that they sent me home to complete primary school in Ermera Vila. I remember my Dad being upset about this.

One moonlit night during the school holidays that year, I was walking with my Dad, the moon, our only source of light in a totally dark landscape. He told me that a man had recently walked on the moon. I remember being amazed as I gazed up at it thinking, what a wonderful achievement that was, and wondering how it was possible. Dad had heard about it on the radio.

It was a year later that school children in Ermera were shown a black and white documentary of the moon landing. Thinking back now, I believe that that night, looking at the moon with my Dad, followed by the documentary of the moon landing, stimulated my interest in science and technology. The comic books that for so long were all I devoured, could no longer hold my interest.

To attend secondary school, we had to move away from home. Initially I moved to a Catholic boarding school for boys in Fatumaca near Baucau; and then in 1974, moved to an Escola Tecnica, a technical school in Dili. It was situated in the centre of Dili just behind the present government offices near the PIDE complex. The PIDE—*Policia Internacional de Defesa de Estado*—had been founded by Prime Minister António de Oliveira Salazar, the notorious Portuguese dictator for 36 years. They were known as 'Salazar's police' and were greatly feared in Timor. It was known that if you were seen to be against Portuguese rule in Timor the PIDE would come for you.

My move to Dili for my schooling more or less coincided with the Carnation Revolution in Portugal so I was a witness to the massive changes this brought to life in Timor as we knew it.

Almost immediately after the coup a group of Portuguese army officers arrived in Dili to decommission the PIDE officers and return them to Portugal. I was in the crowds gathered at the gates of the PIDE complex to watch the removal of this hated remnant of a brutal colonial regime.

The army officers also called public meetings to explain their government's decolonising policy: 'Portugal is giving you your freedom to choose what future you want for your country'. Jose Ramos Horta who was a journalist for the official Portuguese government newspaper, *A Voz de Timor* (The Voice of the Timor People) wrote extensively to keep people informed. The Portuguese government radio station in Timor also informed people in both Portuguese and Tetum of the monumental changes that were being made. My Dad, still living in Fatubessi, owned a radio, so was able to receive all the news and pass it on to others who did not have access to any other source of news.

Another significant sign of changes to come was in November 1974 with the official withdrawal of the Portuguese Governor, Alves Aldeia, and the arrival of his replacement, army officer Lemos Pires.

Some Timorese students who had been studying in Portugal during the lead-up to the coup interrupted their studies to come back to 'help the Timorese prepare for independence', determined to spread the political philosophy they had adopted. Several took up teaching positions and began promoting a socialist agenda. Some became teachers at my school and many of us came under their influence. I well remember former university students who became my teachers: Vicente Reis Sahe, Cravarino, and Hamis.

It was incredibly exciting to be a student at this time of change. With the founding of Timorese political parties, most of us joined the corresponding student unions. The UNETIM was associated with the Fretilin party and LESVALT with UDT. As a member of UNETIM, I began visiting areas in and around Dili, and taught Timorese who were illiterate and had not had any opportunity to attend school, how to read and write—this was a key part of our political activism.

At that time, I was living with my uncle, Custodio Florindo who did not have any political affiliation but, like all other members of my family, had a more conservative political view. He tried to counsel me away from my political involvement with the left-wing student union and, while he did not change my views at that time, out of respect for him, I probably tempered my activities.

During the months that followed, I closely followed the attempts to bring the political parties together. We had hopes that the 'Summit of Macau', scheduled for March/April 1975, would have a successful outcome. However, Fretilin refused to attend because Apodeti, the pro-integration with Indonesia party, had been invited; so unfortunately, without Fretilin in attendance no effective talks could take place.

In July, school holidays saw me leaving Dili and returning home to life in Ermera Vila. Emilia had gone to stay on the Babo property in Ponilala where our sister, Alice and her husband Narciso Babo and their baby Milton, lived. In early August on a family visit to Ermera Vila, Alice told us that her brother-in-law, Joao, needed to go to Dili for business. That suited me as I needed to go to enrol in college for the next year. Alice said that she would ask him to take me with him. For some reason Joao did not call for me which, as events turned out, was probably a lifesaver for me—as will be revealed soon.

On 11 August, the UDT took over authority in Timor in order 'to stop the spread of communism'. In Ermera at the time, I witnessed the capture and imprisonment of the local Fretilin leaders. Since my father was a member of UDT in Fatubessi, he therefore took part in detaining local Fretilin supporters and bringing them to be held in Ermera. One of those he detained and imprisoned was his close friend, Armando Barros.

However, I was about to have another life-changing experience. It was well-known among my family and the wider community that while in Dili, I had been an active member of Fretilin. The day after the UDT takeover, on 12 August, the leader of UDT in Ermera sent his son, who was a friend of mine—accompanied by some UDT supporters, carrying traditional spears and dressed in traditional Timorese dress—to take me away. I remember my Mum being very upset and me being scared for my life as I was marched to UDT Headquarters and placed in detention. It was decided that my punishment was house arrest, so I was returned home to an upset and worried mother and a severe lecture from my father. Punishment indeed!

We later learnt that on 20 August, Fretilin, with the support of Timorese army officers began a counter coup in Dili. Timorese began shooting at each other; and the situation quickly deteriorated. We began worrying about our own safety and that of Alice and her family and Emilia living in Ponilala.

Three days later, my cousin Sergio Galucho, a UDT delegate, fled the fighting in Dili along with his family, travelling in a truck headed for the town of Liquica. It was there that they heard rumours that UDT leaders were already fleeing to Atambua across the border in Indonesia, and that the fighting was now extending to the countryside. They immediately realised that their best chance was to drive to Ermera Vila, stay with family and assess the situation. It would also put them closer to an escape route across the border.

Sergio, and his cousin Joao Roso, and their families—18 already in the truck—headed for Ermera. They had to drive close to Dili and go through a UDT roadblock set up to stop the UDT men leaving. Sergio was able to talk his way through, saying he was just going to his farm up the hill. Once past the roadblock, they continued on to Ermera Vila, arriving around midday.

I remember being excited to see my cousins and, initially, we children all played happily together, having no understanding of the danger surrounding us. I also remember our parents being deep in conversation and there being talk of some UDT leaders who had already left Timor. It seemed that there was a plan for us to leave, too, but not yet.

All this changed when we heard an explosion nearby; a mortar bomb fired by Fretilin forces had exploded in Gleno, a town not far from our village. We were all terrified to realise that now we were caught up in the civil war.

We packed up immediately, then crowded into the truck our cousins came in, which swelled the number of people in it to 48; and joined a convoy of 15 trucks, heading off in the late afternoon. It was soon dark, so we stopped for the night at Vila Maria on the way to Hatolia. Each person found a place to sleep in or around the trucks.

We were later to learn that after we left, an unauthorised UDT supporter threw a hand grenade into the building in Ermera Vila where the Fretilin leaders had been detained, killing and wounding many of the men. I quickly realised that I could so easily have been one of those casualties! Among those killed was my father's friend, Armando Barros. This was to weigh heavily on my father's mind for the rest of his life. It was also the turning point in the revenge killing in the Ermera District. My Dad's boss at the SAPT Coffee Corporation Serafin dos Santos who was the leader of UDT in Fatubessi, was killed, along with other UDT members, while trying to flee Fatubessi.

My uncle, Custodio Florindo, with whom I had stayed when I was at college in Dili, was also the victim of revenge killing. This peace-loving family man who had not taken sides in the political conflict was killed because some of his friends who were UDT members had taken refuge on his farm on their way to Atambua. My uncle's death had a profound effect on me. I realised then that there are many innocent casualties in war, that no one really wins; and from what I now know, in the civil war all political parties came out with blood on their hands—all were involved in the fighting and the revenge killings that resulted.

The journey continued for three days. The truck had blankets but no seats, and with that many people crammed in together, the ride was long and painful, with little food and water. The younger kids were complaining, but somehow, we managed. My Mum and Dad must have been worried about Emilia and her children still in Ponilala. *Will they be okay? Will we see them again?*

During the whole trip, we were wondering what would happen next: afraid that soldiers would find us at any time. I stayed silent most of the time, and just concentrated on helping to protect and care for my younger brothers and sisters. We slept anxiously, camping out and praying that we wouldn't be found.

The second day we arrived in Hatolia where we stopped for one hour. Seeing us and hearing the bad news, the town's people there followed our lead, gathering their belongings and packing into three trucks to join the convoy. On 29 August we stopped in Batucade on the border with Indonesia, where we had to hand over any guns to the Indonesian army officers. Next day we drove for two hours, before the trucks came to a halt and Sergio signalled that we had arrived at our destination: Atambua.

The UDT party leaders and their families from Liquicia, Maliana and other districts, who had already fled the conflict with Fretilin forces, had negotiated with the Indonesian authorities for our asylum in their country. From the day we arrived in Atambua, we gradually realised that we were safe there and so began to settle into a daily routine.

For the first six months, we were with four other families, each with five kids, living in a Catholic kindergarten building. I get the impression that eventually the number and noise of the kids was too much for one of the nuns and she asked the Bishop to move us to a building at the back of the Atambua Cathedral. Next to the Cathedral and the cemetery was a large vacant block which our families soon planted out with vegetables and fruit to meet their needs.

Every day we received a basic serve of vegetables and rice from the Indonesian Red Cross. Never missing an opportunity, the women began baking special dishes which they sold to the people of Atambua. My mother prepared and sold her special Timorese dish of banana fritters which in Bahasa is called *Pissang Goren*. The local people in this area speak a language very similar to Tetum so there were few barriers to communication.

Every day we missed our home and our carefree way of living, but most of all we missed Emilia and Alice, and worried about their safety. The UDT leaders had radios that enabled us to receive some news from home, via the Fretilin-controlled radio stations. But we received no news of Emilia and Alice during the 12 months we stayed in Atambua.

All Timorese males over 18 were employed to rebuild the local airport. I was one of the young men who transported sand up from the river bed to build the base of the airport runway. I remember spending my wages on a much-needed pair of shoes and some shirts.

The Indonesian army arranged for some of the young Timorese men to go with them to help clear Fretilin forces from the areas close to the border, including Maliana and Balibo. When they returned telling us of their successful raids, truckloads of supplies were taken to feed the Timorese who had been 'freed'. We thought that the Indonesian army were helping us to make our country safe for us to return home.

Antonio Pinto, father and grandfather of the Pinto family who had been a commando with the Australian commandos during the Second World War was also in Atambua. He used to listen to the ABC Radio Australia programs and heard of the death of the five Australian journalists, who later became known as 'the Balibo Five'. Less than a month after their death, I went with my cousin, whose truck was hired by the Indonesian army, to take supplies to the people of Balibo.

Initially we all thought that we would return to Timor once the civil war was over. But gradually the UDT leaders and our families began to realise that the Indonesians wanted Timor for themselves. We had hoped that the death of the Australian journalists may have resulted in the intervention of Australia, but nothing was heard!

In due course, the signs of the Indonesian invasion of Timor could not be ignored. Raids by Indonesian soldiers across the borders intensified. The army barracks became a scene of great activity. I have never seen so many trucks in and out of one place. It was on 7 December, with the thundering sound of Indonesian aircraft flying over us, that all our fears were confirmed. Our country was indeed being invaded by Indonesia.

The UDT leaders had brought 23 Portuguese army officers with them to the border town of Batucade, where they were detained. This meant that the UDT were able to use these prisoners as a bargaining tool: the Portuguese government negotiated with the Indonesian authorities for the release of their army officers and the other 1500 or more Timorese who had Portuguese background and who Portugal was prepared to accept. Padre Francisco Fernandes, a Timorese priest who had lived with us in Atambua, took responsibility for arranging for the families to be able to travel to Portugal, working with a Dutch priest and the Dutch authorities.

My thoughts now turned to living in Portugal! Having met Timorese students who had travelled there to study, I knew that they came back with many fresh ideas. The only thing that made me feel hesitant was the fact that we were moving even further away from home; further away from my homeland and from Emelia and Alice. I didn't know what was going to happen. We all missed our home and life in Timor intensely.

The first plane bound for Portugal took the 23 soldiers plus about 70 Timorese. We were on the second plane out which entailed, first an overnight boat trip to Kupang where we were met by a truck and taken to the airport. Then we flew to Bali to board a Portuguese plane which flew to Portugal via Guam and Washington, where we stayed for five hours. While there, we were served lots of food and chocolates. The most amazing experience though was seeing television for the first time ever, and it was a colour TV. Colour television didn't arrive in Portugal for several more years!

Our family arrived in Portugal in 1976 and stayed for six years. Landing in Lisbon at night for the first time was very exciting. I was 18 but had never seen a big city! At the airport we witnessed people returning from two other Portuguese colonies—Angola and Mozambique—where civil wars were raging, as well. The authorities didn't call us refugees, they referred to us as *Retornados*, returning citizens, which was somehow more inclusive.

We had learnt that a few months after the *Revoluacao do Cravos*, there had been another coup in Portugal—the 'Revolt of the Captains'. This time no shots were fired and the military, led by Captain Ramalho Eanes, took charge. By the time we arrived two years after this, he had been elected and we had the opportunity to vote for him for his second term.

Portugal was so different from everything we knew in East Timor: there were no dense trees, mountains or hills; and there were lots of concrete houses and buildings. Despite the differences, for us, it was incredible. Everyone was so peaceful and happy in comparison to the situation we had left. Honestly, it was heaven compared to the anxiety and fear we had experienced before we left Atambua knowing that our beloved country had been invaded by the Indonesians;

and knowing that Emilia, Alice and her children were still there and in danger.

On our arrival, the Red Cross arranged prefabricated accommodation at Quinta da Graca refugee camp, which we welcomed even though the buildings were not completed. Initially, there were no internal walls, so parents used blankets as wall dividers between families.

All meals were served in a huge dining room which was formerly the home of a wealthy businessman whose property was called Quinta da Graca. We all attended the school at the camp, continuing our education from where we left off in Timor as it was the same curriculum. A year later we moved to Balteiro camp, about two kilometres away, and into completed pre-fabricated timber houses. During the decolonisation period, Portugal took in more than one million refugees from their former colonies.

In 1978, we received news that Emelia and Alice were alive, following their surrender to the Indonesian army. My father registered their names with the Portuguese Red Cross and requested that they be reunited with their family in Portugal. We were very disappointed when Alice's husband would not agree for the family to leave Timor.

In 1979 at the age of 21, I married Adriana Varudo, and our daughter Lelia, was born soon after. We moved in with Adriana's family in the Balteiro refugee camp while I worked for two years as an apprentice fitter and turner. Later on, we moved to a government apartment in Alfragide and in March 1982, our son, Nelson, was born.

In the middle of the year before that, our father suddenly became ill when painful cysts developed on his neck. It was a very sad time for all of us as the cancer developed. He passed away just five months later in November 1981, never having seen his daughters or Timor again. At that time, the only way we could let Alice and Emilia know was by telegram.

Although we had made a good life in Portugal the family began discussing migrating to Australia. We had a cousin living in Sydney and we were told that 'the prime minister is letting us go to Australia because we have a cousin living there who has arranged to sponsor us'. The first of our family to go was Luzia who flew to Sydney in March 1982 and lived with my cousin Joao Rosa, a fellow escapee in the truck that fateful day when we fled Emera Vila and headed across the border to Atambua.

A few months later, my sister Rosa, and I, said goodbye to Mum and the rest of the family when they flew to Australia. By the time they arrived in Sydney, my sister Luzia had met her partner and was living in Melbourne, so Mum and the family were welcomed at the airport and then immediately taken on the ten-hour drive down south to Victoria. When asked recently about what she thought of being taken on a day-long journey immediately on arrival in Australia, she commented, 'I thought that this is what people in Australia did, since it is such a huge country!'

Soon after Mum left Portugal, Emilia was reunited with Rosa and me. It was such a joyful reunion for us to see and hug our little sister once again after all those anxious years, to know that she was finally out of danger. But we were all very sad that Alice and her family could not be with us as well. My family were sponsored by Francisco Florindo, another cousin living in Melbourne, so we arrived in June 1983.

My Mum is an amazing person. She has supported her family while herself experiencing dangers and many challenges. She adjusted to life during the civil war, life in exile in Atambua, life in her adopted country of Portugal and finally, migrating to a new life in Australia. She was delighted—as were all of us—when Alice and her four kids came from Timor to visit and then decided to stay. With her family once again reunited, Mum remains the centre of the family; and we all gather at her home for a meal at least once a week. She supports her family who still remain in Timor, including providing a house in Dili for her sister. And she visited Timor regularly until recently when her health would not allow her to travel.

◈◈◈

On reflection, I appreciate the wonderful beginning we had in Australia, with family already here to welcome us, to accommodate us and to provide us with such valuable guidance. Having an established Timorese community helped us to quickly and more easily feel at home; it was in the community where we could attend Saturday parties and where many young people met their future partners for life. Most importantly for me, a ready-made soccer team was there for me to join, which meant training on Wednesdays after work and playing on Saturdays and Sundays.

The Florindo family has dedicated this story to the memory of their cousin, Sergio Galucho, who passed away in June 2017. We want to thank him for his wise and brave decision to travel through the danger and the horror of the civil war, to collect us and take us on a three-day drive to safety. We acknowledge that Sergio saved 48 lives on that journey. We know of family members and friends who did not have this chance to escape, who were among the thousands who lost their lives during the civil war.

Also, our heartfelt thanks go to my cousin, Joao Rosa, for sponsoring my Mum and family to Australia. And thank you, Australia, for allowing us to settle here and for providing initial financial support for the first couple of months it took for me to find a job. I had learnt a little English when at school in Portugal, so have managed to gradually master this, my fifth language. My siblings and I have all married and continue to enjoy life as our families increase. We have suffered sadness with the death of my sister Luzia, and of Janine the daughter of Irene, but continue to be a close, loving family.

We haven't forgotten East Timor and the family and friends who remained there. My first visit was in 1999 following the referendum. I went into Dili on a program organised by Pat Walsh, activist and long-term supporter of independence, when the Australian Occupational Forces moved in. I spent 10 weeks working for NGOs, including Oxfam and the Red Cross, helping with translations and interpreting. I have made several more visits since then and tried to support the young people I know to develop opportunities for employment. Some of my attempts haven't been as successful as I had hoped; I have learnt that I need to spend more time living in Timor with my family and friends if my support is to provide them with any longer-term benefit. As I get older and think about retirement, my plan is to spend the Australian winters in Timor. Maybe then I can be of some real use!

Do I identify as a Timorese, a Portuguese, or an Australian? I can truthfully provide the following answer. In Australia I feel Australian, my children are Australian, and I am accepted as an Australian. In Portugal I know I have Portuguese blood, I speak the language and I am accepted as Portuguese. I really love Timor but when I am there and meet strangers, they consider me a foreigner until I speak fluent Tetum, then I am welcomed back as a Timorese. How lucky am I to be able to identify with all three.

Alice and Emilia's story

Emilia was 13 years old in July 1975 and was spending the school holidays staying in Ponilala with her married sister, Alice, when the rest of her family—her parents, her brothers and sisters, and her cousins, were forced to flee from the family home in Ermera Vila and seek temporary refuge in Atambua, over the border in Indonesian Timor (Irian Jaya).

Emilia loved spending time in Ponilala with Alice, her husband Narciso Babo and baby Milton. Narciso's father was the *Liurai*, the traditional leader of Ponilala, and the Babo family owned a large piece of land.

Milton was such a happy baby and loved Emilia carrying him around the house and out into the garden; and Emilia enjoyed spending time with her sister, sharing conversations away from all their other brothers and sisters while helping with the baby, the cooking and gardening.

Ponilala was a very small village, very quiet, where nothing unusual happened; and where they only received news of their family in Ermera Vila when someone visited. While staying with Alice, sometimes Emilia did miss the everyday hustle of the family crowding into the house for meals, and the family dog, Café, and his barking at noises in the night.

In early August Alice, baby Milton, and Emilia visited their parents in Ermera Vila. During that visit, they arranged for Jose to go with Joao, the brother of Narciso, on his business trip to Dili. Jose needed to re-enrol at the technical college for the next academic year. When, at the end of that visit, Alice and Emilia farewelled their parents and siblings, they could not imagine that they would not see them all again for several years.

It was 11 August when they returned to the Babo home in Ponilala. The political conflict had intensified and the Babo family, as supporters of UDT, were part of the *Movimento anti comunista*, MAC, which was detaining Fretilin leaders and supporters.

When Fretilin took over Ermera Vila in the last week of August, Narciso and all the men of UDT, fearing for their lives, attempted to flee to the border.[9] Left behind, Alice, Milton, Emilia, all the other women, children and old people from Ponilala were rounded up and moved to Ermera Vila by orders of the Fretilin leaders. It was thought that the 'prisoners' would be easier to control in the town. When they reached Ermera Vila, the two sisters found that the shopkeepers had all left, leaving the place looking like a ghost town. They wept when they approached the deserted family house but were delighted to be greeted by their family dog, who promptly jumped up on Emilia, licking away her salty tears. Alice and Emilia could only hug each other, wondering whether they would see their family again.

They stayed at the house of a cousin in Ermera Vila for two weeks, by which time one of the Narcisco brothers,

9 Fretilin was targeting the men who were members of UDT, not women and children.

who was a member of Fretilin, came from Dili and, to their great relief, took them to stay at the Bishop of Dili's house in Lecidere where they could feel safe again.

Meantime, while trying to flee the Fretilin forces, Narciso had been captured and taken back to Ermera Vila and, along with other UDT men, was placed in detention. Fortunately for him though, his previous training as a nurse meant that he was freed from detention to work in the Ermera Hospital where he worked alongside a professional nurse attending to wounded Fretilin forces.

While there, Narciso managed to arrange for his family to join him in Ermera Vila. Emilia remembers being unhappy, however, about having to leave the comparative safety of the Bishop's compound and return to a place where they had experienced such terror.

It was during October that they heard from the local people that Indonesian soldiers were coming across the border to move Fretilin forces off the land, but at this stage there was no sign of any Indonesians, so they had no idea what was happening to their people in other districts.

Then on 7 December 1975, Emilia remembers very clearly that, 'Large numbers of planes flew over. Looking up in the sky as a child, I had no idea who was flying these planes and where they were going. The adults were saying they were Indonesian planes that were on their way to Dili. I remember their fear, which for us children translated into terror. We wondered what it all meant and what would happen to us.'

They didn't have to wait long: within a week, people fleeing from Dili arrived in Ermera Vila bringing the news that the Indonesian army had invaded and had now fully occupied Dili; and that Fretilin forces continued to resist the invading forces. For months they heard these stories but did not see any sign of it.

When Indonesian forces finally closed in on Ermera Vila, the whole population, including Alice, baby Milton and Emilia, were forced to follow the Fretilin guerrilla force up into the mountains. Narciso was allocated work in an improvised hospital in the village of Abat near Fatubessi, and in that year, Alice's second child, Sonia, was born. The family managed to survive eating corn, tapioca, sweet potatoes plus anything they could find in the bush. Indonesian military planes would regularly fly over, looking for the guerrillas. This meant that even the lighting of fires for cooking was too risky. Life was both difficult and full of danger.

Then capture.

'It was the second birthday of my daughter Sonia—12 May 1978. Gunfire shots were coming from everywhere. Everyone, including Narciso and Emilia, ran as fast as they could to escape. I crouched, holding onto my two little children, praying for a miracle.'

Alice's prayers appeared to be answered because when the Indonesians couldn't see any guerrillas there, they stopped shooting, and marched all the women and children to the village of Oileu close to Fatubessi, where they spent the night. Next morning, they all had to walk uphill to Fatubessi, where they spent another night. On the third day, they were forced to walk another 10 kilometres to the village of Aifu near Ermera Vila. Exhausted, Alice carried her two-year-old Sonia while an Indonesian soldier carried four-year-old Milton.

Soon after their arrival, an Indonesian soldier called Beni began chatting to Alice, telling her that he had been on duty in Atambua. He asked if she had a sister called Luzia who may have fled to Atambua, saying that he had met a young woman who looked exactly like her. Alice was so relieved to hear this news from such an unexpected source: to know that all her family had escaped from Ermera Vila and were now safely over the border.

She was later taken back to Ermera Vila where she was detained for two days and questioned about the movements of Fretilin. On her release she stayed at a relative's house for two weeks afterwhich a leader of the Apodeti (pro-integration with Indonesia) arranged for her, Milton and Sonia to be taken to Dili and reunited with Narciso's family. Safe again for the time being, Alice must have worried about the safety of her husband and Emilia.

Emilia now tells the story of what happened to her when the Indonesian soldiers ambushed them on 12 May 1976.

'Suddenly there were shots flying everywhere. Everyone fled into the bush and I remember running as fast as I could to keep up with the others, and to escape the Indonesian soldiers. I was terrified. I cried and cried when I heard the news that Alice and the children were captured. We had heard so many stories about the bad things that the Indonesian soldiers had done to other Timorese. What would they do to them? Now all my family were gone, and I was alone.

'We stayed in the bush, running away when we heard or saw soldiers looking for us. Narciso surrendered after a few months as he wanted to find his wife and the children, but a group of us—women and children—stayed on the run, eating what we could find, always hungry. After many months of starvation, we knew we could not survive any longer, so the whole group surrendered.

'The Indonesian soldiers took us by truck back to Ermera Vila, the older women hiding the young girls under their long skirts to protect them from the men. We stayed in Ermera a few days and it was here that I received the first of some wonderful news of my family. Alice, Narciso and Milton were all safe and now living in Dili. I was overwhelmed with emotion and thanked God for this news.'

The same Apodeti leader who had arranged for Alice and the children and later, Narciso, to travel to Dili now arranged for Emilia to be taken there, too.

'Life was a blur as I travelled to Dili. My mind only cleared when I arrived and was in the arms of my beloved sister, and hugging little Milton and Sonia. It was then that I heard the rest of the wonderful news: my Mum, Dad and all my family were alive and well, and living in Lisbon, in Portugal. I have never felt such relief and such joy.'

Life settled into a different routine once again. Emilia returned to primary school, but this time it was an Indonesian school and she was introduced to the language of Bahasa. It was 1978 when she began her study of the Bahasa language and completed the final year of primary school, before moving on to SMP junior high school in 1979.

The following year she was working in a shop when a friend, who knew she was separated from her family and that she was keen to be reunited, met an Indonesian Red Cross official and told him Emilia's story. She asked if her name was on a list of missing family members. Later on, that Red Cross official returned from Jakarta with the great news that Emilia's name was indeed on the list and that she should begin to prepare to be reunited with her family in Portugal. Alice was also keen to join her family but her husband, Narciso, did not want to go.

It was while Emilia was preparing to leave Dili to join her family that they received the telegram telling them their father had died. The two sisters were heartbroken, crying inconsolably; it had been so many long and incredibly difficult years since they had seen their father, and now he had died, so far from home.

'It was so sad to have to say goodbye to Alice and her children not knowing whether I would ever see them again. As we flew out of Dili I thought of how my sister was now to be completely separated from all members of her family.

'But the plane was filled with other Timorese who were also to be reunited with their families. So there was such a buzz of excitement as we all anticipated seeing loved ones again, that it lifted my spirits, and I began to wonder what life in Portugal would be like.

'It was February 1983 when I arrived in Lisbon, to be met by Rosa and Jose. It was only then that I heard the news that Mum and the others had left Portugal a few months earlier and were now settled in Melbourne. While happy to be reunited with Rosa and Jose, my thoughts were, "Why am I here? I came to Portugal to be reunited with my family and now most of them are so far away in Australia". My greatest wish for so long had been that we would finally be able to live together as a family again.'

A year later in 1984, my wish was granted when I was welcomed to Melbourne by my Mum. I hadn't seen her since July 1975, nine years earlier, when I was only 13. Now I was 21. In all my teenage years, I did not have my mother beside me. It was not until August 2016 that I took the opportunity to return to East Timor, accompanied by my Portuguese-born husband. Visiting the places and seeing the houses where I had spent my childhood was such an emotional experience for me. Memories of family and friends—who had mostly moved away, many to other countries—flooded in. I noticed that there was less vegetation than how I remember it as a child. Some important buildings remain: the chapel in Fatubessi where my Mum and Dad had married was still standing, as was the school and church we attended in Ermera Vila.

Timor is in my heart always. I was born there and have good memories of my early childhood. And I feel so grateful that we were able to survive more than two years of physical danger and starvation.

Australia is a paradise for me. I have a loving family, and looking back on what I have gone through in my life, I can say with feeling: I am lucky to be alive.

A TRIBUTE TO THE TRUCK

The following families were on board the truck when, on the 27 August 1975, they were forced to flee from Ermera Vila to Atambua to escape the civil war.

1. Sergio and Celeste Galucho and their children—all living in Melbourne
2. Andre and Azinha Machado and their children—all living in Melbourne
3. Joao and Lolita Rosa and their children—all living in Sydney
4. Nazario and Fatima Andrade and their children—some living in Melbourne, some in England and some in Timor-Leste.

This tribute in poem form was written by Kimberley Lofthouse, a student at Gleneagles Secondary College, 2016, Melbourne.

Darkness. Fear.
The smell of people pressed against each other. The glare of the sun as it rose and fell, day by day. People whispering to each other, sharing their lives with each other.

Stay positive.

The old mattresses, kept there for the children's comfort. The feeling of being squashed; the feeling of being trapped. Camping out each night, sleeping in constant fear of being discovered. Leaving as soon as the sun rose.

Stay positive.

The smell of tainted air, combined with the aches and pains of rough road travelling. The constant bumps and rattles of the truck and the squeals of younger children.

Stay positive.

The fear of soldiers stopping them—even finding the children. The trust they had in their cousin. He could get them through this. He would get them through this.

Stay positive.

Soon, they'd be out of the dangerous country. They'd reach wherever they were going… soon.

Stay positive.

They might have nothing but the clothes on their backs and the sparks in their eyes, but they would survive this. They would survive. They could make it. This was a good truck. It would get them there. Good truck. They'd be safe.

Stay positive.

'Stay away from the sides!'

'Don't be seen!'

'I'm worried about the children…'

'Are there soldiers here?'

Footsteps echoed near. Huddle. Stay down and stay together.

Stay positive.

Stay together. Try to keep that spark going. Don't let the fire die.

Huddle for warmth. Keep this cold, old truck alive and as happy as possible.

Stay positive.

They would make it. They would get out of this alive. They were almost there. The truck would get them there. They would make it.

Stay positive.

'Do we have enough fuel to make it?'

The buildings in the distance, children peeking over the side of the truck cautiously.

Call them back down. They haven't made it yet. It wasn't safe yet.

Stay positive…

The families becoming closer, sticking together. They were so close to the border.

The truck had stopped. Was it soldiers? Had they been found?

The atmosphere felt… different, somehow. Had they made it?

Stay positive.

Their cousin's knock rang out on the side of the truck.

'We're here. You can come out, but stay close.'

Climbing out of the truck, feet touching the ground for the first time in many, many hours.

Making sure everyone was there, that they hadn't lost anyone.

The truck had saved their lives.

They had stayed positive.

And they had made it.

Napoleon Family

Manuel Napoleon

I was born in the Ermera district of East Timor in 1960. I am the eldest child in the family and have a brother, Jose, and a sister, Maria. We came to Dili to live with Grandma after Dad's work contract with the Agriculture Department on the coffee plantations in Ermera ended early in 1965. Grandma's house was in Taibessi, south-east of Dili. Later in the year, the family moved to Lahane, south of Dili, to a modest three-bedroom house with one living room, a kitchen, a bathroom and storeroom, and verandas at the front and back. There were up to 13 people in the household: Grandma, Uncle Nico, Auntie Ceu and her three children—me, Jose, Maria—and adopted family Ines, Antonio and Amelia. There was also another young boy who helped around the house for a wage. The breadwinners for the household were my Dad, Luis, who worked on board ships, my Auntie Ceu who was a social worker, Uncle Nico, who worked in the Communications Department, and my Grandma who had a pension.

When my parents separated, our Mum decided to go back to Ermera, while we continued living with my grandmother who was able to offer a better standard of living. Grandmother was a very strong personality. Widowed in her late thirties, she had had to raise her five young children alone: my dad

Luis, Uncle Nico and three aunties (Lurdes Chuxa, Rosentina Babo and Ceu). Given her survival skills and character, my Grandma always made sure we had food and clothes, and that we carried on with our schooling. Hardship was not visible to us, maybe because we were kids.

I started my primary education at Balide Catholic School and then I moved to the public primary school of Eng. Canto Resende. Most of the older kids attended school and shared home duties after school: finding firewood for the stove and general cleaning around the house. In 1971, I started my junior high school education at the Escola Tecnica Professor Silva Cunha in Dili. However, because I failed the first year at that school due to too many absences (I was wagging), as a punishment from my Dad, I was placed into a Catholic boarding school.

Soon after this, however, my father tragically drowned when the cargo ship that he was working on sank on the way to Bangkok. With the loss of my Dad, suddenly our finances became very difficult for my grandmother to manage, especially because we did not have any right to Dad's pension.

Despite this, as education was so highly valued in our family, my grandmother somehow found a way for me to stay at the boarding school until the end of 1974. That school still bears the name of Externato St Jose and is situated just south of Dili not far from my Grandma's last residence. From there, I continued my schooling in Dili at the Technical School. The boarding house was managed by Padre Monteiro, an Indian priest who served in Timor-Leste for most of his tenure. One of my teachers was a Timorese priest, D. Martinho Lopes, who later became the first Timorese bishop during the early Indonesian occupation.

It was hard for me to adjust to not living at home in the beginning, but as the time wore on and our family's income was so low, I could see that I didn't have a choice, eventually moving back to Grandma's.

When the civil war started in 1975, my Grandma, auntie, sister and younger cousins had to evacuate to a protected area in Farol—a seaside suburb in Dili. I was left in the house with just my 12-year-old-brother and my nine-year-old cousin; and Grandma's strict instructions to look after the house (and them, of course!) until further notice. As the fighting intensified, we decided to go looking for Grandma, auntie and the girls. My uncle Nico had been missing for days and we did not know where he was, but we knew that we had to find a safer place.

As we walked towards the beach, there were regular exchanges of gunfire between the armed men from the two warring political parties (UDT and Fretilin) in the streets around us. When we reached the waterfront, we decided to walk along the foreshore to the wharf. Suddenly, some Portuguese soldiers seemed to come out of nowhere and grabbed us. Pointing to one of the warehouses in the port, they said, 'Quick. Get in there, boys!' Looking back now I would say that we were very, very lucky. They probably saved our lives…

But back to that day: when we dashed into the warehouse, imagine our surprise to see a lot of people inside—mostly women and children; and much later, to everyone's overwhelming joy and relief, finding out that our Grandma, auntie and my cousins were there also. The warehouse was our refuge for a week, although it was very hard because there were food shortages and the added anxiety of not knowing where we would go next.

One afternoon, we were told by the Portuguese soldiers to jump into barges that were ferrying people fleeing Dili to a large Norwegian cargo ship called SS *Lloyd Bakke,* which was moored just outside Dili Bay. The ship headed for Darwin late that night, carrying our family and more than 1150 others, through the night.

Seeing Darwin on the horizon the next morning was unbelievably exciting and such a relief. I could not wait to disembark as the ship was a mess of rubbish and exhausted people. When we got closer, the ship was boarded by the Australian authorities (Navy, Customs, Quarantine and Immigration) for clearance before it docked at the wharf.

I was filled with many different emotions, not knowing what to expect; for a time my head felt as if it was spinning because I thought we were on the move again. Sometime during the clearance process, the family became separated. But eventually, after a good half day, we were all finally given permission to leave the ship.

Travelling along in the bus from the wharf, we were surprised to see a great deal of devastation and destruction, as if there had been a war there as well. We were told that it was caused by Cyclone Tracy which had almost completely destroyed Darwin nine months earlier on Christmas Day, 1974. We also found out later that the ship which brought us to Darwin was actually in the vicinity because it was providing assistance to the people affected by the cyclone.

The bus took us to another wharf where we boarded the cruise ship RHMS *Patris* which was moored in Darwin also to accommodate the cyclone victims of the Northern Territory. As we boys settled in, free from our Grandmother's influence, I found out that some of our group's members were split up. After we had been warmly welcomed by the Red Cross on arrival, and then sent to our respective accommodation: some to the Australian Air Force base and others to live in schools around Darwin which had not re-opened since the cyclone.

A few days later, the authorities were able to reunite us, and a week later, we were told our group plus others had been chosen to fly to Melbourne on a TAA[10] flight sometime in September. This was to be another journey for us. On the way to airport, I was excited and apprehensive at the same time, as it was my first time on a plane. However, all the stress and horrible experiences in the last weeks and months must have left me completely exhausted: within minutes of take-off, I fell into a restless sleep, only waking when I could see the sunrise through the window. Then I became a bit confused seeing many clouds underneath the plane and thinking they were snow, and that we were heading to a very cold place.

Landing in Melbourne, we were again transferred to buses, and were amazed that Red Cross staff were there with blankets for everyone. The buses transferred us to the terminal where another terrifying experience was looming—escalators! It felt so unnatural to be able to move up and down without moving my own feet.

10 Trans Australian Airlines was one of the two major domestic airlines in Australia at the time. Founded in 1946, it merged with Qantas in 1992.

My first impressions on the journey to our temporary residence at Midway Hostel in Maribyrnong, was of a highway full of cars and a landscape that was constantly changing. Once at the hostel, more blankets and clothing were distributed by the Red Cross and other charity organisations before we were allocated to our accommodation.

Our time at the hostel was very exciting because we were sharing our living space with other refugees from South America, mainly Chileans, and other countries too, and we were met with challenges every day. However, after listening to the Latinos talk Spanish, a language which is very similar to Portuguese, we had an advantage connecting with them.

We settled in very easily with a lot of support from the Social Services, including from a charming old Catholic nun called Sister Paula, who I remember well. Sister Paula asked my Grandma if she would let us kids go away for the weekends and school holidays, to encourage friendships in the community by introducing us to Australian families. She also thought it would relieve Grandma from the pressure of having so many children (there were nine of us) under her care.

As a result of this excellent scheme, we were introduced to two big, beautiful Dutch families. Jose, Maria and I went to the Schalkwyk family in Broadmeadows; this modest, caring family of nine were more than happy to add extra people to their family. Ines, Amelia and Tony went to the Dewitt Family in Faulkner.

Grandma used to get a bit nervous about us all going off for weeks at a time, always wondering if somehow someone was going to adopt us without her knowing. I think that losing us briefly when we were separated into different accommodation in Darwin, left her with a fear of that happening again, but permanently. One time she called us back from one of our homestays early, before school holidays had ended, just out of that fear of losing us.

The hospitality and sense of humanity we experienced with the Schalkwyk family was the highlight of our stay with them and it will live with me for the rest of my life.

Sister Paula also enrolled me at St John's College in Braybrook where I was put into Year 10. That was a challenge for me as my English language was not, to me at least, good enough. The other less exciting aspect was my experience with Vegemite which I thought was disgusting! At the time, peanut butter or Vegemite sandwiches and an apple were the only available school lunch options.

Being the only Timorese kid in this college I must admit it, was not easy despite all the help that I was getting; and I did try hard to learn. My brother, sister and cousins and the rest of my family went to a state school near the hostel.

Two months later, we were told by my aunt and Grandma that our group was to move again, this time to Enterprise Hostel in Springvale where there were more Timorese refugees. So we had to start all over again: new home, new school. Moving from Midway to Enterprise was not as difficult in terms of settling in because our previous experience gave us an advantage. By then, too, we had a better grasp of the language and, just like before, we played communal games like soccer, table tennis, pool and darts that were fun and for which you didn't need a lot of language.

This time, I went to the same school as the other Timorese children, Westall High School, which also had special English classes for migrants and refugees. I was there for the next ten months. Assimilation with other migrant and refugee communities at the hostel was quite easy, and we made friendships that have lasted until today.

Our family of ten (excluding my auntie, who chose to live in Richmond Housing Commission flats) was given a Commission house with three rooms and a bungalow. This helped us to make a new start, but despite all the support from government agencies and the local community, we felt nervous about facing the outside world. Travelling to Westall High School every morning just became harder and harder, especially during winter.

The lack of personal financial support became a factor for me in deciding whether to continue at school or find a job at this point. When an opportunity at Repco Bicycle Company in Clayton came up through the contacts of a friend from Enterprise Hostel who was the same age as me, I did not hesitate. A week later, I found myself on an assembly line fitting front wheels on bicycle frames.

During this time, my thoughts always turned to my family left behind in Timor (especially Mum and others) and, of course, Timor, itself. The possibility of me returning seemed increasingly remote now that we were becoming more established in the suburbs of Melbourne which made me very sad.

It was such a surprise then, when a friend of Grandma's, an Indonesian lady called Imelda, came to visit with exciting news. She had evacuated with us a few years ago, but had recently gone back to visit Timor. While there, she was contacted by my Mum and the rest of the family so was able to tell them that we were safe and in Australia, which the International Red Cross later confirmed for them, also.

After a few months saving up, I moved to a boarding house in Clayton so I could make the journey to work more easily. Here, I met some Timorese boys living in a house nearby and, despite our little differences, I moved in with them for the next couple of years.

Some of the boys went their separate ways and created a life for themselves. The younger boys stayed together and moved to a house in Oakleigh. I moved out to Mentone where I found a new job which I stayed in for the next eighteen years working as a welder and boilermaker at the Ramler furniture company in Cheltenham.

Although the Indonesian occupation of East Timor was always on my mind, I decided to become an Australian citizen. My son, Edgar, was born in 1985 at Sandringham Hospital and I got married a year later. Having a young family provided new challenges again in dealing with the future. After my son finished high school, I applied for an Australian passport so I could visit my mother.[11]

Most of the pro-Indonesian news was coming from the mainstream media in Australia, but I was hearing news of human rights abuses from some friends in the clandestine resistance movements in Timor which began to be reported in Australia, too.

---

11 The Indonesian Government would only grant us tourist visas if we travelled on Australian passports.

I had initially intended to continue living in Australia, but over the years the idea of going back to my homeland was always at the back of my mind. I finally made up my mind to return even though it was still occupied by Indonesia and in 1989 just before Christmas, I landed in Dili with a group of Timorese friends from Melbourne, full of a mixture of emotions and a lot of anxiety. We just did not know what to expect on our arrival, knowing from contacts on the ground and the international media of the regime's brutal human rights record towards the anti-Indonesian Timorese. What will the Indonesians make of us who had fled and returned?

After clearing immigration without a problem, I went to stay at the house of a relative of a friend in Dili for a few days to organise my trip to see Mum in Ermera; she was not expecting me. The day came to make the trip and again, after more security checks, I travelled by road for three hours with a relative, all the way to my mother's house.

As I arrived at the front of the property and looked up the hill at my home, I couldn't contain my tears. Still crying, I walked up the hill towards the house where my Mum and my maternal grandmother were staring at me in disbelief and wonder, as if they were dreaming. I remember that it took a bit of time to hear my mother's voice, with other members of the extended family crowding around joyfully when they heard the news of my arrival.

It was such an emotional day that even now when I remember that scene, I am moved again to tears that seem to rise out of somewhere deep down inside me. It took a few more days for her to adjust to the fact that it was indeed me who was staying with her, reminiscing about the sad and happy times.

Within the bosom of my family again and, knowing that I would be heading back to Australia, I didn't want to jeopardise any good opportunities that would harm future trips. I wanted to learn more about the struggle of the people against the Indonesian regime but at the same time I was careful to avoid placing my family in a risky situation with the authorities.

When it came time to leave, my family and friends decided they wanted to see me off in Dili. At the airport, I told my Mum that I was coming back again, not knowing that I would travel back four more times until 1994.

Four years later, in Melbourne, my feisty Grandma died which was very sad—she had had such a big impact on so many lives and had saved so many of the family. With her passing meant that we suddenly had the challenge for our 1975 group, of maintaining the bonds and staying in contact with each other.

On December 1999 after the massacres and chaos that followed the independence referendum, I returned to East Timor with my son, Edgar, who was fourteen years old at the time. We travelled on an Australian navy ship—HMAS *Jervis Bay* from Darwin under the International Forces control, trying to find my Mum again, as we had lost contact with her during the last horrific six months in that battered country. Arriving at the same port where I left in 1975, to the burnt ashes of the city of Dili, destroyed by the militias with the help of Indonesian military, I found my Mum on that same day at the place where my family had taken refuge, my

Mum's coffee plantation. She was so shocked and thrilled to see us and to meet her grandson, Edgar. But I guess it was a bigger shock for Edgar, coming from a wealthy country to see a devastated East Timor, the country his father had always yearned for, but now in ruins.

◈◈◈

Eventually, after four years of long and, of course, emotional consideration, my wife, Maria, and I moved to Timor-Leste; this time for good. Edgar continued his further studies, living in Melbourne with his grandparents and aunties from his mother's side.

D-Day came in December 2004. Maria and I had packed up everything that we needed into a dual-cab ute which we drove all the way to Darwin. From there, we took a boat to Dili, accompanied by Mojo, our German Pincher puppy, who enjoyed her new home for ten years, until her death.

Arriving in Timor to live, again, was another chapter into the unknown. Naturally, our family back in Melbourne were not sure if we had made the right decision, given all the circumstances.

A lot of dreams in the first six months suddenly became a reality when I found a job as a tour guide for a local tour company. This inspired me to start my own tour company. Then, sadly in 2006, my marriage collapsed, followed by political and military crises in Timor where at one stage, I thought that I would be a refugee again... That's all in the past and I am here to stay though there are still challenges facing my beautiful country.

Despite our separation, Maria and I have managed to keep the business, Eco Discovery, going until the present day; and in this small way, we feel we are making a small difference to the country and the people of Timor-Leste.

Australia will always be my second home, but my heart is here in Timor-Leste.

Thank you, Australia.

It's not the years in your life that count, but the life in your years.

Maria Napoleon

I was three months old when we moved from Nunutali—a small mountainous village in the Ermera District of East Timor more than three hours' drive along rough tracks and roads to Dili—to live with my father's Mum, Grandma Rosentina Napoleao. All my family were at Grandma's: Mum, Dad and my two older brothers, Manuel and Jose. My three cousins and some other children were also living with her; we had moved so we could all have a chance for a better education and a better life.

My Dad, Luis Napoleao, worked on a ship whose captain was married to his sister, so they were mostly away at sea. My Dad had visited what seemed for us to be exotic destinations like Australia, Singapore and many other places that I could only dream about. I remember hearing of the adventures of some family members who travelled on the ship with my father and brought back amazing things from these foreign ports. The only sea adventure that my brothers and I had—for us, wonderful and memorable—was a day visit to Atauro Island, a beautiful place off the coast from Dili, which is now an eco-tourism destination for Timorese and international visitors.

Every time Dad returned from sea, he would bring home exciting presents that most people even in Dili would not have seen: apples and pears individually wrapped that looked amazing and had a wonderful and different taste; films and a home projector so we could have film nights at home with friends and family, watching 'The Three Stooges', 'Laurel and Hardy', amongst others, before television came to East Timor (in 1978). He also brought home furniture from Singapore; I remember each piece being individually wrapped in plastic, which was never removed!

I was three months old when my mother, Maria Clotilde Soares, left us in Dili to go back to live in Nunutali. How I missed her! In those days, the Portuguese were very much the ruling class and Grandma identified as Portuguese more than Timorese. I always sensed that she felt superior to my Mum who was Timorese, and often wondered if that was why Mum left us.

Although Grandma was very strict with us children, life was good in Dili; a different life and a higher standard of living was granted to us—more so than if we had stayed in Ermera. Can you imagine! We had our own running water, a shower and a toilet. While we lived like Portuguese, we had many daily responsibilities too. We each had our own piece of ground for vegetable growing and our own chickens and ducks to feed and care for. The ground had to be dug to plant the corn and other vegetables, but my brothers, typical boys, were sometimes very lazy and only spread dirt on top of the weeds. They were punished when Grandma found out, though! From a young age, I can also remember washing clothes, which the boys didn't have to do—it was definitely only the girls' responsibility.

Although we were not well-off, we lived among families who were. Our neighbour across the road was the Australian Consul. Sometimes there would be parties at their home and we would sneak across the road, lie on the ground and look in the windows, amazed with the beautiful clothes and the food. A girl in my class at school who lived next door was the daughter of the chauffeur to the Governor, and he brought the car home each day. For us, that was incredibly exciting as there were very few cars in Dili then.

My auntie, Maria Do Ceu Napoleao, daughter of my Grandma, lived with us, too. She worked at the Red Cross, helping mothers with babies who had come down from the mountain and other remote villages to have their babies checked and vaccinated. Sometimes on school holidays, we went with Auntie to the Red Cross to help out, to feed the little children and help in any way we could. We loved holding the babies, and washing and feeding them; but you had to be on the alert as Timorese babies don't wear nappies!

In 1973 my Dad decided it was time to retire from life at sea, announcing that this would be his last voyage. My auntie took me to the wharf to say goodbye; I felt so special being there to see him off. As he walked away, he suddenly stopped and came back for another hug.

How could we have known that he would never return, that that was the final hug I would ever have from him? On that, his final trip, the ship sank, and he drowned, along with all his shipmates. I had only known my Dad for eight short years.

The day we received this tragic news was profoundly traumatic for the whole family. I remember Jose and I being collected from primary school and returning home to Grandma overwhelmed with grief. My Grandma, the solid rock of the family, was screaming out at the loss of her son, her daughter, and her son-in-law, all drowned at sea. Life changed dramatically for us from that day. Money was now only available for necessities, and there were no more fancy presents from overseas.

But for all of us Timorese, life was about to change dramatically on a larger scale as well, in 1974, after the Carnation Revolution in Portugal. For me as a young child, I had no idea what was happening, all I knew was that life had become very scary. Trucks loaded with people would drive around Dili with loudspeakers calling 'Go for Fretilin!'; and at night we could hear gunshots. Everywhere you went, you could hear people talking more and more about the politics, and fighting.

It was on one ordinary day. I was playing with my cousins and my Grandma was in the shower when my auntie came running into the house yelling, 'We have to leave NOW!'.

My auntie's boyfriend was in the Portuguese army, so he had advance warning that the area of Dili where we lived was no longer safe, even for civilians; he had come with his jeep to collect us. Grandma said that she wasn't going to leave her house and all her things. At which point, to my horror, my auntie took her boyfriend's gun and said to Grandma, 'Come now, or I'll kill you!'

On Grandma's orders, my brothers and my boy cousin stayed behind to look after the house while the rest of us were driven to the Carrascalão family, who were Grandma's friends, where we stayed for several days. It was a regular house, close to the wharf, so the adults thought we were safer there because we could escape easily by boat if necessary. But as things got worse, with more frequent gunshots and fighting in the streets, we sought safety in a warehouse on the wharf where there were many other families sheltering.

Although my auntie had stopped going to work and was living with us in the warehouse, she continued to support other families where she could, including vouching for people who, having fled their homes in panic, had no identification papers. Fortunately, her long-term work with the Red Cross meant that she was widely known and trusted by the people and the authorities.

Life at the wharf was both scary and exciting. Food was in short supply but we all shared what we had. Those whose houses were nearby would return to tend their gardens and animals and collect eggs when there was a pause in the fighting. During that time, we were able to taste and use the many goods still stored in the warehouse: that's where we were introduced to Coca Cola for the first time, helping ourselves from the stacks of slabs. While we spent a lot of time sitting around, I do remember that there were also some stereos stored there so we were able to listen to music.

Eventually, Manny, Jose and my cousin joined us at the wharf and recounted their recent adventures. They had decided to leave our home in Lahane when fighting in the area escalated, taking refuge at the UDT camp. The morning they left the camp to return home was the day Fretilin revolted against UDT rule and began arresting and killing some of the UDT supporters. The boys had hitched a ride on a water tanker driving in the direction of our house when at one of the major intersections, the truck was waved down by armed Fretilin supporters. They told all the kids to go home and then arrested the driver. The boys walked home, but seeing how dangerous the situation was becoming, later that day, they made their way to the wharf and joined up with the rest of us kids.

Things must have got worse, but as kids we didn't notice. A Norwegian container ship came into port and agreed to take people to safety. Portuguese soldiers who were with us at the wharf, took responsibility for selecting who should board the small boat to be taken to the ship. However, those with darker skins were not selected: my three fair-skinned cousins and their fair-skinned mother—who had one Portuguese parent—were allowed but we were not. Fortunately, a family friend, a person of some influence, vouched for us, allowing all of us with darker skins to board: Grandma, my auntie, my two brothers, my three other cousins and three additional children who had also lived with Grandma. It was the Portuguese authorities who objected to our dark skin not the Norwegians.

As the small boat left the wharf, a bomb was thrown which just missed us; we would have died if it had been thrown accurately. On board the ship we stayed on deck and managed as best we could. I vividly remember babies crying and strong winds blowing. Milk and bread were only available for babies and infants, so we had a very hungry and cold 10-hour journey across the ocean to Australia.

Arriving in Darwin, there was much confusion: our group was separated which meant that we ended up in three different camps. For us children, it was very exciting being in a new country, and also being separated from Grandma and her strict rules, if only for a few days.

One of the first things I remember upon reaching our camp was all the food laid out before us. I had never seen so much food in all my life: fresh fruit sitting spread on very long tables, and meals three times a day. Because we had been hungry for so many weeks, at first, we put extra food inside our clothes just in case we were once again without enough!

We had a lot of fun enjoying a freedom we had never known in our first few days at the RAAF Airforce Base. Without Grandma there, we had no one to tell us to go to bed, so we stayed up late watching planes and helicopters landing and taking off. Later, I learnt that all this activity was the relief effort supporting Darwin after Cyclone Tracey, but at the time it felt like being in a movie.

Altogether again and reunited with Grandma, we were soon on our way to Melbourne where we settled first into the Midway Hostel. The highlight of our arrival was being taken into a huge building where clothes and shoes were stacked on tables; we could choose whatever we wanted. Life was exciting, like an adventure; the food was different, there were clubrooms where you could play table tennis and snooker. There was even a pinball machine, but while my brothers and boy cousins were allowed to play there, Grandma wouldn't let us girls go anywhere near it.

Finally, we moved to the Enterprise Hostel in Springvale, from where, each day we were taken by bus to Springvale South Primary School. Our lunches were supplied by the hostel. I knew only a few words in English and there was no one to help us with learning it, but I tried to fit in. Like the other kids, I looked forward to having some money to buy a Wagon Wheel biscuit or a few coins to buy a bag of lollies. I have an indelible memory of one teacher, Mrs Godfrey, who was so tall she seemed to tower over us—she gave me a wack for chewing gum in class. Needless to say, I never did it again and I still recall her name.

Many years later, when living in Australia, a group of us was talking about our escape from Timor and the bomb-throwing incident. To our amazement the person who threw the bomb identified himself right there. He explained that at that time, he was young, a member of Fretilin and got caught up in the conflict. Following the Indonesian invasion, he had fled to Portugal and later migrated to Australia. Yet, here we were meeting again under quite different circumstances. How strange is life!

I had never had the chance to bond with my mother, but when my twins were born in 1992, I felt an overwhelming need to visit her. She was still living in a small house in the same mountain village in the district of Ermera. East Timor had been occupied by Indonesia since 1975—seventeen years. Leaving the one-year old twins and their older sister with my husband, I travelled with my brother Manny, and spent two weeks there.

Mum was only expecting a visit from Manny, who had visited her previously, so you can imagine her surprise when she saw me, the daughter she hadn't seen for more than twenty years. We hugged for a long time.

Fortunately, I still spoke Tetum so we were able to communicate with each other. Being a mother myself, who could not fathom ever leaving my children, I couldn't help asking her the question soon after my arrival: 'Why did you leave us?' She replied that she missed her home and her land where she had many fruit trees, chickens and pigs and many vegetables; also, she missed her family and friends. She didn't admit to feeling inferior to Grandma, but I still suspect that that was the real reason.

While staying with Mum in Nunutali, we witnessed what it was like for Timorese families under Indonesian occupation. Indonesian soldiers stayed with us all the time we were with Mum, making sure we weren't involved in any political activities while there. They would help themselves to whatever food was available and would steal the best fruit from her trees. Mum showed her anger towards them, but there was not much she could do about it.

We were followed everywhere by Indonesian army officers, or other officials, and sometimes taken in for interrogation. If we travelled to another town, we were stopped and interrogated. When we drove to my husband's family, an Indonesian army jeep followed us all the way. Even when we stopped in Bali on the way home, we were still watched and followed. Very stressful! I did learn later that the Indonesian authorities suspected my brother of working for the resistance movement, and they were correct.

My next visit was in 2003 when my husband and I took our three children to meet their grandmother. East Timor was finally independent so we enjoyed a happy and stress-free visit this time. Staying with Mum was wonderful because although they didn't share a common language, our children got to know their grandmother and we could see how much joy that brought to her. However, being unused to the country, we misjudged the weather in the mountains of Ermera and found the first night very cold; my poor husband had to travel back to Dili next day for more blankets.

Mum visited Melbourne in 2008, and by then over 65, it was her first visit outside Timor. While she enjoyed her stay, she found life in Australia hugely different from her village life in East Timor. She loved spending time with her grandchildren, but there was still no common language which made it very hard for her. Eventually, she began to miss her family and friends in East Timor, her routine, her small coffee plantation, her farm, and her animals. So, after a three-month stay, she was ready to return.

◈◈◈

I love East Timor and we plan to visit Mum next year and in the future. I missed having my mother with me for most of my life, but living with Grandma in Dili at the start of the civil war, enabled us to escape the conflict in my homeland and settle in Australia.

I am grateful that Australia accepted us. I realise now that I identify as an Australian who comes from a Timorese background. This is probably because I was only a child when we came, so I became an adult and married here, and my three children were born and educated here. I do enjoy celebrating our Timorese culture among our family and sharing it with our many friends.

A Brief Chronology of East Timor's Key Historical Events since Portuguese Colonisation

For almost 500 years, East Timor was a Portuguese colony.

1518

One of the first Portuguese to visit the island, Duarte Barbosa, wrote: 'There's an abundance of white sandalwood, to which the Muslims in India and Persia give great value and where much of it is used'. Dutch administrator, Schulte-Nordholt, also refers to the interest it represented for the Portuguese. Other products were exported such as honey, wax and slaves, but trade relied mainly on sandalwood.

1942-1945

Japanese occupy East Timor throughout World War II; 40,000 East Timorese die during the war.

1945

Post-war, East Timor reverts back to Portuguese administration.

May 1, 1959

Armed uprising against the Portuguese administration based in Wato Lari and Wato Karbau, near Viqueque. The Portuguese raised a militia in the neighbouring area of Los Palos to put down the rebels.

April 25, 1974

The left-wing coup, the *Revoluação do Cravos* (the Carnation Revolution) takes place in Portugal, resulting in the first step towards East Timor's decolonisation.

May 1974

Decolonisation begins with the (Portuguese) Governor of East Timor announcing general elections and calling for the establishment of political parties.

October 1974

Indonesia begins a covert destabilisation operation, including subversive radio broadcasts from across the border in West Timor (Irian Jaya).

March 1975

General elections begin.

July 1975

FRETILIN wins 90% of the vote in local elections.

October 1975

Indonesia begins attacks across the border from West Timor. On 16 October, five Australia journalists (later called the Balibo Five) are killed in the remote border village of Balibo.

November 28, 1975

FRETILIN declares 'The Democratic Republic of East Timor'.

November 30, 1975

The Balibo Declaration inviting Indonesians to liberate East Timor is signed by compromised UDT and APODETI leaders.

December 7, 1975

Indonesia launches a full-scale air and sea invasion of East Timor.

December 12, 1975
The UN General Assembly calls on Indonesia to withdraw.

December 22, 1975
The UN Security Council condemns the invasion.

February 1976
60,000 East Timorese have been killed since the invasion began.

November 1976
More than 100,000 East Timorese have died.

July 1976
President Suharto declares East Timor to be Indonesia's 27th Province.

November 28, 1977
The UN General Assembly rejects integration and calls for an act of self-determination for East Timor (and the UN General Assembly continues to call for self-determination for the people of East Timor by passing resolutions until 1982).

June 10-11, 1980
An attack on Dili is mounted by East Timorese resistance forces.

May 4, 1982
Elections are held in East Timor in which the official Indonesian party, Golkar, win 98.8% of the vote.

November 3, 1982
UN General Assembly again condemns the annexation by Indonesia and calls for an act of self-determination. The UN

Secretary-General is instructed to initiate discussions with 'all concerned parties'.

1983

During the 1980s, Xanana Gusmão makes a number of attempts to come to a peaceful settlement with the Indonesian invaders. Along with war-weary Indonesian troops, localised ceasefires are negotiated, and in March a regional cease-fire is agreed upon by Gusmão and Indonesian military representatives. But in August the Kraras massacre signals the end of the cease-fire. In September, a state of emergency is declared and a new Indonesian offensive, Operation Unit, is launched.

August 18, 1985

Australian Prime Minister Bob Hawke recognises Indonesian sovereignty over East Timor on behalf of his Labor Government.

September 24, 1985

After again deferring action on East Timor, the UN oversees the first formal contacts between Portugal and Indonesia since the invasion.

December 9, 1985

Australian and Indonesian governments announce that they will jointly develop the petroleum reserves in the Timor Gap.

1987-1988

In a reorganisation of the resistance structure, Gusmão declares FALINTIL (the armed wing of the resistance) a non-partisan 'national' army. In 1988, he relinquishes membership of the political party FRETILIN, believing the fight for a free East Timor transcends political loyalties.

He establishes the National Council of Maubere Resistance (CNRM) and is declared leader.

October 1989
Pope John Paul II visits East Timor and a huge demonstration in Dili signals the beginning of a phase of urban political demonstrations organised by the emerging youth resistance.

Late 1991
The Resistance begins to prepare for the visit of the Portuguese Parliamentary Delegation, planning a formal ceremony.

October 28, 1991
Two youth are killed on the steps of a Catholic church in Dili.

November 12, 1991
Hundreds of Timorese in Dili participate in a funeral procession for their two friends killed in the church in Dili. Along the route to the cemetery, banners are unfurled, protesting against the cancellation of the visit of the Portuguese Parliamentary Delegation, while others call for freedom for East Timor, in front of the Western journalists who were in East Timor preparing for the visit of the Portuguese parliamentarians. The Indonesian troops descend on the funeral march and open fire on the unarmed students. Hundreds of Timorese are trapped inside the cemetery wall, and are killed. The journalists smuggle out the videotapes of the funeral march/ demonstration and the events are shown on television worldwide, becoming known as the Santa Cruz massacre.

November 1992
Gusmão is captured by the Indonesian soldiers.

February-May 1993

Gusmão's trial in Dili. He is sentenced to life imprisonment and refused to make a statement in his defence. Ma'Huno becomes the leader of the resistance movement in East Timor but is soon captured. Konis Santana then becomes leader of the resistance.

1993

Youth resistance begins campaign of entering foreign embassies in Jakarta.

January 1994

UN Special Rapporteur on East Timor visits Gusmão in Cipinang Prison in Jakarta to formulate new initiatives for the next round of talks between Indonesia and Portugal.

June 1995

The UN sponsors talks between pro- and anti-independence East Timorese (The All Inclusive Intra-Timorese Dialogue—AIETD)

July 1995

Half of the East Timorese signatories to the 'Balibo Declaration' retract.

August 1995

Gusmão is put in solitary confinement for writing a letter to the UN, sponsored Beijing World Women's Conference.

March 19-22, 1996

Second UN-sponsored Intra-Timorese Meeting. The final statement does not include the demands of the external Timorese resistance, which includes the release of Xanana Gusmão.

June 27, 1996

Eighth round of talks between Indonesia and Portugal; the only resolution is to build a Timorese cultural centre in Dili.

October 1996

The Australian Senate passes a unanimous motion supporting East Timor's self-determination.

December 1996

The Nobel Peace Prize is awarded jointly to José Ramos Horta and Bishop Belo, the Catholic Bishop of Dili from 1989-2002.

October 1997

Third and final AIETD Talks.

April 1998

The National Timorese Convention is held in Portugal, which establishes the CNRT (The National Council of Timorese Resistance) to replace CNRM. This non-partisan national organisation is the new umbrella for Timorese resistance. It brings together different political nationalist organisations and unanimously elects Xanana as President.

May 1998

Indonesian President Suharto resigns following student pro-democracy pressure from the Indonesian public.

August 5, 1998

Agreement between Indonesia and Portugal at the UN to undertake, under the auspices of the UN Secretary-General, negotiations on a special status based on a wide-ranging autonomy for East Timor.

November 20, 1998

Portugal suspends talks with Indonesia after reports of a massacre.

January, 1999

The Australian government changes its foreign policy and support's East Timor's right to self-determination.

February 1999

Gusmão is moved to house arrest in Jakarta. He warns of further possible violence and calls for international armed peacekeepers in East Timor.

March 3, 1999

Indonesian President Habibie announces that if, in a 'process of consultation', the majority of East Timorese rejected autonomy in favour of independence, Indonesia would grant independence. The CNRT and international solidarity groups, together with several countries, begin to call for a ceasefire, disarmament and Indonesian troop reductions.

May 5, 1999

Agreement between Indonesia, Portugal and the UN to put a special autonomy framework to the East Timorese people through a 'popular consultation' and for the UN to establish a UN Mission, UNAMET, in East Timor to implement the referendum. The Indonesia government is made responsible for maintaining peace and security in order that the popular consultation could be 'carried out in a fair and peaceful way in an atmosphere free of intimidation, violence or interference from any side'.

June 11, 1999

The UN Security Council formally establishes UNAMET through the end of August 1999. In resolution 1246 (1999) adopted unanimously, the Council endorses the Secretary-General's proposal for a mission including up to 280 civilian police officers to advise the Indonesian Police, as well as 50 military liaison officers to maintain contact with the Indonesian armed forces. The Council stresses again the responsibility of the Indonesian government in the maintenance of peace and security in East Timor to ensure the integrity of the ballot and the security of international staff and observers.

June 18, 1999

At a press conference in Dili, SRSG Ian Martin says that continuing violence has forced tens of thousands of East Timorese from their homes, creating a 'serious obstacle' to preparations for the vote on the future of the Territory.

August 24, 1999

Indonesian authorities assure UNAMET that they will try to create a secure environment. Members of the UN Security Council express strong concern at the continuing campaign of intimidation and violence in East Timor and call on the parties to fulfil their commitments to disarm and store their weapons.

August 26, 1999

The UN Security Council extends UNAMET's mandate until 30 November. In a unanimous vote, the Council adopts Resolution 126 (1999) endorsing the Secretary-General's proposal to restructure the UN Mission in East Timor for the interim phase after the 30 August vote.

August 30, 1999

Referendum is carried throughout East Timor, and at key sites for Timorese living abroad. At least 95% of those registered, vote.

September 2, 1999

Pro-integration militias, at times with the support of elements of the Indonesian security forces, launch a campaign of violence, looting and arson throughout the entire Territory.

September 4, 1999

Results of the ballot are announced: 78.5% of East Timorese vote for independence by indicating the CNRT flag on the ballot (and thus rejecting the proposed special autonomy arrangement with Indonesia).

September 1999

The pro-integration militias, with substantial Indonesian military backing, engage in a period of uncontrolled terrorism. An unknown number of East Timorese are killed, and over 200,000 are forcibly displaced into West Timor and other parts of Indonesia. Gusmão is released amidst military slayings in East Timor. He takes temporary refuge in the British Embassy and then flees to Darwin after receiving death threats. From there he goes to the UN in New York to appeal for immediate armed intervention by the international community, as well as to seek humanitarian assistance for the Timorese.

September 15, 1999

The UN Security authorises an Australian-led multinational force, INTERFET, to restore peace and security in East-Timor. Gusmão returns to a devastated East Timor and makes emotional pleas for all Timorese to return home, to forgive and to rebuild.

October 25, 1999

The United Nations Security Council, by resolution 1272 (1999), establishes the United Nations Transitional Administration in East Timor (UNTAET). The Mission comprises three main components: governance and public administration; humanitarian assistance and emergency rehabilitation; and a military component with an authorised strength of up to 8950 troops and 200 military observers. UNTAET is led by the Special Representative of the (UN) Secretary-General (SRSG) Sergio Vieira de Mello.

October 27, 1999

The Consolidated Inter-Agency Appeal for East Timor, led by the World Bank, is launched in Geneva to request $199 million to meet humanitarian needs through June 2000.

October 31, 1999

The last Indonesian troops leave East Timor.

November 27, 1999

The SRSG signs the first of a series of legal instruments setting out the terms of UNTAET's administration of the territory.

December 2, 1999

The SRSG signs Regulation 1999/2 on the establishment of the National Consultative Council (NCC), a 15-member joint East Timorese-UNTAET body, through which the representatives of the people of East Timor can actively participate in the decision-making process during the transition period.

December 3, 1999
UNTAET establishes, by regulation 1999/3, a Transitional Judicial Service Commission comprising five individuals, three East Timorese and two internationals.

February 23, 2000
INTERFET formally transfers its military command of East Timor to UNTAET.

March 27, 2000
The East Timorese Police Academy is established.

April 28, 2000
The East Timor Postal System commences operation.

May 12, 2000
The Dili District Court commences its first public proceeding.

May 30, 2000
At the opening of the Conference on Reconstruction, UNTAET proposes a period of co-governance between UNTAET and East Timor prior to a full transfer of authority.

June 21, 2000
UNTAET and CNRT agree on a new composition and structure for consulting with East Timorese on legislative and policy matters, called the National Council. The National Council has 33 members, which includes 13 representatives from the districts, seven representatives from CNRT and three

representatives from other political parties. Its other members represent youth, women's groups, and non-governmental organisations, as well as the Catholic, Protestant and Muslim communities, professional and farmer's associations, the labour movement and the business community. All members, including the chair of the NC are East Timorese.

July 12, 2000

The NC adopts a regulation establishing a Transitional Cabinet comprised of four East Timorese and four UNTAET representatives.

The first 50 graduates of East Timor's Police Academy officially take up their functions as police officers.

September 6, 2000

Three UNHCR staff are murdered in Atambua, West Timor, following an attack by armed militias on the UNHCR office.

September 8, 2000

The UN Security Council adopts resolution 1319 which insists 'that the Government of Indonesia take immediate additional steps, in fulfilment of its responsibilities, to disarm and disband the militia immediately, restore law and order in the affected areas in West Timor, ensure safety and security in the refugee camps and for humanitarian workers, and prevent cross-border incursions into East Timor'.

September 12, 2000

The East Timor Transitional Cabinet approves the establishment of the East Timor Defence Force (ETDF) with former FALINTIL soldiers representing the core of the 3000-strong force.

March 17, 2001
UNTAET begins civil registration.

June 9, 2001
The East Timor resistance umbrella organisation CNRT is dissolved to make way for a range of political parties to participate in the upcoming election for a Constituent Assembly.

July 15, 2001
The Transitional Cabinet and the National Council are dissolved and elections begin for an 88 member Constituent Assembly, whose mandate will be primarily to draft the constitution of East Timor.

August 30, 2001
Election for a Constituent Assembly, East Timor's first democratic elections.

September 6, 2001
FRETILIN is declared the winning party, with 57.3% of the vote in East Timor's Constituent Assembly elections.

September 20, 2001
24 members of the new all-East Timorese Council of Ministers of the Second Transitional Government are sworn-in.

October 22, 2001
The President of the Constituent Assembly signs a resolution approved by the Assembly that UNTAET hand over sovereignty to elected Timorese government institutions on May 20, 2002.

October 26, 2002

The first East Timor Defence Force battalion is formally inaugurated.

October 31, 2002

The Security Council endorses Secretary-General Kofi Annan's recommendations that the United Nations continue its role in East Timor after the territory's independence next year, stressing that a premature withdrawal of the international presence could have a destabilising effect in a number of crucial areas.

January 31, 2002

The UN Security Council unanimously adopts resolution 1392 (2002) extending the mandate of UNTAET until 20 May 2002.

March 22, 2002

East Timor's Constituent Assembly approves and signs East Timor's first Constitution.

April 14, 2002

East Timorese presidential elections are held. Francisco da Amaral, Deputy Speaker of the Constituent Assembly and Xanana Gusmão stand as the only two candidates.

April 17, 2002

Xanana Gusmão is announced as President-elect of East Timor after capturing 82.7 per cent of the vote in the presidential elections.

May 20, 2002

East Timor becomes an independent nation. Xanana Gusmão is formally sworn in as the first President of East

Timor. The first Cabinet of the Democratic Republic of East Timor is sworn in, with Mari Alkitiri as Prime Minister. The National Parliament votes unanimously for East Timor to join the United Nations. This resolution is made before many leaders of the world, including the UN Secretary-General, in Dili, East Timor.

Published with permission courtesy: Australia East Timor Friendship School Project Booklet, Alola Foundation

www.ingramcontent.com/pod-product-compliance
Ingram Content Group UK Ltd.
Pitfield, Milton Keynes, MK11 3LW, UK
UKHW021827270726
14058UKWH00001B/10

9 780987 381101